# Nanaimo

Heritage
House

# Nanaimo

## The Harbour City

### Goody Niosi and Terry Patterson

Credits for photos other than those by Terry Patterson:
Eve Reinarz, page 112; Nanaimo Archives, pages 17, 19, 20, 22, 26, 28, 29, 32, 35, 63, and 64.

HERITAGE HOUSE PUBLISHING COMPANY LTD.
Unit #108 – 17665 66A Ave., Surrey, BC V3S 2A7

Library and Archives Canada Cataloguing in Publication

Niosi, Goody, 1946-
    Nanaimo: the harbour city/Goody Niosi ; Terry Patterson, photographer.

ISBN 1-894384-56-3

    1. Nanaimo (B.C.)—Guidebooks.  2. Nanaimo (B.C.)—Pictorial works.
I. Patterson, Terry, 1954-  II. Title.

FC3849.N35N56 2004              917.11'2          C2004-902852-9

Cover and book design by Nancy St.Gelais and Darlene Nickull.
Edited by Ursula Vaira.
Printed in Canada

Heritage House acknowledges the financial support for our publishing program from the Government of Canada through the Book Publishing Industry Development Program (BPIDP), The Canada Council for the Arts, and the British Columbia Arts Council.

The Canada Council | Le Conseil des Arts
for the Arts | du Canada

BRITISH
COLUMBIA
ARTS COUNCIL
We acknowledge the support of the Province of British Columbia
through the British Columbia Arts Council

# Contents

# Acknowledgements

So much goes into the production of a book like this, and I have many people to acknowledge and thank.

First, thank you to Peter Cruise at P.B. Cruise Booksellers who gave me the idea, and thanks to Thora Howell, who agreed that Nanaimo needed a book like this and urged me to go ahead and do it. Thanks to Rodger Touchie, my publisher, who said "yes" to the project and got behind it.

A big thank you to Terry Patterson, who is an amazing photographer. When people asked me about the book long before it was ready, I consistently told them, "It may not read like much, but it sure is going to look good."

I want to say a huge thank you to the Nanaimo Archives and especially to Christine Meutzner. The historical section would never have come together without her. Thank you also to the Nanaimo District Museum and to Ocean Explorers Diving for help in underwater stills.

Thank you to the *Nanaimo Daily News* and to sports reporter Michael Rhode, who helped with the section on sports, a subject about which I am pitifully ignorant.

The editors at Heritage House were immensely helpful. A book like this is a team effort, and it could never have happened without everyone pulling together. A collective thank you to Darlene Nickull, Vivian Sinclair, Ursula Vaira, Karla Decker, and Nancy St.Gelais.

My biggest thanks go to Nanaimo, a city that has welcomed me since the day I arrived eight years ago and whose talented, kind, and generous people make the heart of this city beat so strongly.

# Beautiful Nanaimo

For centuries, Nanaimo's sheltered harbour, rugged shoreline, protected islands, accessible beaches, and numerous rivers and lakes have made it a gathering place. The word Nanaimo is an anglicized form of the Coast Salish word *Snuneymuxw*. Some historians say it translates as "great and mighty people," while others believe it means "gathering place," and there are good arguments for the latter.

The Snuneymuxw were the first to call this area home. They found food, fresh water, and winter shelter among the islands and inlets. The first European settlers were miners brought to the area by the Hudson's Bay Company in 1850. While the Company specialized in the fur trade elsewhere in the country, in Nanaimo it discovered not only an abundance of wildlife, but also some of the richest coal seams on the west coast of North America.

For the next 100 years Nanaimo was the destination for miners and their families from England, Wales, Scotland, the United States, Finland, Italy, and other European countries. The Chinese arrived and brought their own rich heritage, and Nanaimo became a mélange of nationalities. The people who came to Nanaimo fell under the spell of its natural beauty and created a solid, permanent community.

*The ferry from Nanaimo provides fast, reliable, and economic service to the Lower Mainland.*

*The Port Theatre attracts professional acts from all over the world. It is also a favourite venue for community groups and the home of the Vancouver Island Symphony Orchestra.*

*Fishing boats tie up in Nanaimo Harbour's commercial-boat basin, while cruise ships,
larger vessels, and pleasure crafts are able to moor at the 600-ft. Visitng Vessel Pier.*

Service clubs, drama groups, and musical societies thrived. The Nanaimo Opera House, built in 1888, was the venue not just for operas, but also for musicals, plays, revues, and vaudeville shows.

When oil replaced coal as a fuel, Nanaimo made the transition from coal town to mill town. In 1950, Harmac, a giant pulp and paper mill, became Nanaimo's major industrial employer and absorbed many of the miners into its workforce.

The next wave of settlers began arriving in the 1970s, and people continue to settle in this idyllic spot. These modern-day settlers come for the incomparable climate, pristine wilderness, abundant wildlife, tranquil waters, friendly people, arts and culture, and jewel-like oceanfront setting.

Nanaimo's setting is unique. The city rises in the shape of an amphitheatre, with its beautiful waterfront taking the spotlight below. The historic downtown and old city form the dress circle, a short distance from centre stage. Farther back, Malaspina University-College climbs up the lowest flanks of Mount Benson, the green giant whose ridges encircle Nanaimo's western limits.

Boaters and sailors have long recognized Nanaimo's protected harbour as one of the prettiest in the world, and the city has become the central transportation hub for Vancouver Island. It is here that ferries, cargo ships, and barges arrive from the mainland. Roads lead west to Port Alberni, Tofino, and the wild beauty of Long Beach; south to the pretty towns of

Fisherman's Market in Nanaimo's harbour is a convenient place for boats to tie up and sell their catch of the day, which can range from fresh halibut to plump prawns and fresh Coho salmon, all caught in local waters.

Shack Island and nearby Piper's Lagoon add greatly to Nanaimo's history and the lore of its surrounding areas.

*Nanaimo's attractive harbour lures a wide variety of sailboats, from sleek racing craft to homemade live-aboards.*
*The* Faireheide *sails out of Schooner Cove, one of the many marinas in and around Nanaimo.*

*Killer whales are frequently spotted in Georgia Strait. Ferry passengers on the*
*way to Nanaimo often keep a sharp lookout for these magnificent creatures.*

Ladysmith and Chemainus, the impressive Malahat drive, and the enduring charm of Victoria; and north to the windswept white-sand beaches of Parksville and all the way to Port Hardy and the rugged northern tip of the Island.

Nanaimo is also a centre for the arts and has attracted a notable population of artists and artisans, many of whom are justly famous throughout the country. The Port Theatre, an 800-seat performing-arts centre downtown, is home to the Vancouver Island Symphony and hosts such touring groups as the Royal Winnipeg Ballet and other world-class performers, such as Nanaimo native Diana Krall and Dame Cleo Laine.

Nanaimo is also well known as a city of festivals and special events. It has the distinction of being the Canadian city with the longest-running celebration of Empire Days— since 1867—in honour of Queen Victoria's birthday. Each year Nanaimo's downtown hosts the Vancouver Island Children's Festival, an entertainment extravaganza for children and families, and, of course, the famous and occasionally notorious World Championship Bathtub Race. In June, world-class racing yachts compete in the Cadillac Van Isle 360° International Yacht Race, which circumnavigates Vancouver Island.

Nanaimo attracts hikers and mountain bikers to its diversity of trails and kayakers to its protected waters. Divers come from all around the world to explore the world's largest artificial reef and the renowned Dodd Narrows and Gabriola Passage.

Nanaimo is a modern-day playground and a thriving city, highly competitive in the emerging technology and tourism fields. But it is also a city that pays tribute to its history and deeply honours those who gathered here even in the days before its story was recorded.

*Known for its sheltered harbour and wide rage of marine services, Nanaimo attracts boaters from up and down the west coast of North America.*

# The Beginning

How the Snuneymuxw arrived in this verdant land is shrouded in legend, but there is some early tribal history that is etched in stone. At Petroglyph Park in the south end of Nanaimo are carvings thought to be 2,000 to 10,000 years old. Little is known about these carvings or about this place. The rocky rise of land near the water may have been a sanctuary for the Snuneymuxw. Some historians believe it may have been a sacred place where west-coast shamanism was practised.

The Snuneymuxw had their first contact with White people when the Spanish arrived in 1792. Francisco Eliza and José Maria Narvaez had seen the east coast of Vancouver Island in 1791, and Eliza had named the passage leading to Nanaimo Winthuysen Inlet after a Spanish rear admiral. On June 15, 1792, Dionisio Galiano and Cayetano Valdes, who were completing surveys of the area, came to Winthuysen Inlet. The Spaniards were charmed and recorded in their logs: "Under a clear sky a pleasant country presented itself to our view. The varied and brilliant green of some of the trees and meadows, and the grand roar of the waters dashing upon the rocks in various corners charmed our senses."

The Snuneymuxw were suspicious, and the Spanish had great difficulty winning their confidence. On one occasion, men in 39 canoes surrounded the ships with weapons at the ready. Despite this distrust, a small amount of trading took place.

*The Bastion stands guard over the harbour in the old colour-postcard above. The watercolour on the left by Lieutenant Panter-Downs is a depiction of the coaling station in 1859.*

# The Snuneymuxw

Departure Bay and the downtown harbour were indeed gathering places for the Snuneymuxw Nations. There were five families, or tribes, that came together here in winter and held potlatches by the rivers emptying into the sheltered harbour.

During days of good winter weather, the Snuneymuxw fished and hunted near their villages, but for the most part they lived on food they had stored during the summer. The chilly, rainy weather and the winds of January and February made travel uncomfortable and often impossible. During these times, the Snuneymuxw told stories, passed on their legends to the young people, and danced. They did not create great totem poles like the Haida or Tlingit, but their other carvings and their celebrations rivalled any on the West Coast.

As the days grew longer in March, the people began to supplement their diet with duck, salmon, and cod. In April hunters went after deer and elk, and the fishermen returned to the halibut fishing grounds. This was also the time to fish for herring, which were so plentiful that the Snuneymuxw caught them by the tens of thousands.

In May the women began gathering camas, wild carrots, and rushes, and toward the end of the month they began to dismantle their winter longhouses in preparation for moving to their summer homesites.

The Snuneymuxw lived a life well adapted to their habitat and they thrived. In the 1850s a census showed a population of 900 to 1,000 in the area. Fifty

*This image in stone, carved by A.G. Johnny, is positioned near the Swy-a-lana Lagoon in tribute to Swy-a-lana, the legendary eldest son of the first man in Nanaimo.*

years later, only 158 had survived the ravages of various European diseases.

Today the Snuneymuxw population numbers 1,300 people, 65 percent of whom live on four small reserves on the shores of the Nanaimo Harbour and the Nanaimo River, with the remainder living off-reserve in Nanaimo, Victoria, Vancouver, and Seattle. The Snuneymuxw, like many First Nations in British Columbia, are in treaty negotiations with the provincial government and are planning for a brighter economic future with particular emphasis on sustainable forestry products and shellfish farming. The Snuneymuxw economic development office is also exploring partnerships with local private enterprise and is a member of Nanaimo's Economic Development Group.

*The age of sail lingered in Nanaimo harbour long after the first steamers arrived at the coal docks.*

The Spaniards landed to refresh their supplies of food and water and after three days, during which they explored the area, they set sail again. But they left a lasting heritage in the place names they left behind. The Gabriola Island ferry still docks in Descano Bay. Indeed, the island itself is named after Punta de Gaviola. Gabriola Island's fantastic Malaspina Galleries, carved by the ocean out of rock, and Malaspina University-College, which rises up the foothills of the Westwood Ridges in Nanaimo, take their names from the Italian explorer Alexandro Malaspina, who was in the service of the Spanish.

But the Spanish did not settle Nanaimo—that was left for the English, when they were lured to the area by the promise of coal.

The Hudson's Bay Company was well aware of the potential value of new coal seams. Joseph MacKay, a clerk at the Victoria post, reported a large outcropping of good-quality bituminous coal above the high-water mark on the beach in a sheltered harbour. James Douglas, governor of the crown colony of Vancouver Island, made the trip that summer by canoe. He was impressed with the find and quickly took possession of the coal beds in the name of the Hudson's Bay Company.

Douglas brought in miners and placed John Muir in charge of coal operations. MacKay organized the building of seven log huts, a store, and loading docks for coal ships. The surveyors and construction workers toiled hard, but it was nothing compared to the hours those first miners put in. They started work before dawn and continued until well after the sun went down, and on September 10, 1852, the first shipment of 480 barrels of coal left Nanaimo bound for Victoria on the schooner *Cadboro*. On September 30, the *Recovery* loaded 1,391 barrels.

The new settlement was far closer to Victoria than any other source of coal. The First Nations people were friendly and eager to work in the mines, and the coal was near the surface and readily available. The only trouble was that other tribes, particularly the Haida, would come down from the north on raids. So in 1853, the Hudson's Bay Company started building a blockhouse, or bastion, that could shelter the White settlers and command a far-ranging view of the harbour. Evidence shows that although the building of the Bastion began in 1853, it was probably not completed until 1854 or 1855. Clearly, the early settlers were concerned about attack, but not worried enough to be in any hurry to protect themselves.

# The Bastion

The Bastion still looks out over Nanaimo's Harbour and is the last remaining fort of its kind in Canada. The view from the Bastion's top storey takes in Protection and Newcastle islands, sailboats catching a summer breeze, and floatplanes buzzing into the sky. This sturdy structure, originally used as a trading post, now stands guard like some ancient centurion over Pioneer Plaza, with its coffee houses and chic shops.

But step through the massive wooden door on the first floor, and you'll be transported back into another age. In the hush of the dimly lit interior you can almost hear the scratching of the clerk's old steel-nib pen as he records the trades of warm Hudson's Bay blankets and sacks of potatoes, flour, and oats. The second floor contained the defence arsenal and trap doors, which hid cannons primed and ready to fire. But raids were few; in fact, the guns were never used for defence and were fired only for salutes on ceremonial occasions or to prove to the Natives that they could do damage.

The third storey of the Bastion was the largest—large enough to shelter all the settlers in the small outpost in case of an attack. Records show it was used only once, when there was fear of a canoe raid by the fearless Haida nation of the Queen Charlotte Islands.

The village was named Colvile Town in honour of Andrew Colvile, the governor of the Hudson's Bay Company. He predicted a coal boom and advertised in England for more skilled miners.

Those miners and their families arrived in Nanaimo in 1854. The population of the new settlement shot from 21 to 75, and the village began to assume the look of a permanent little town. Mark Bate, the mine manager, became the city's first mayor in 1860, when Colvile Town officially became known as Nanaimo.

By 1862 Nanaimo's reputation as a coal-mining town was firmly established; it was shipping 18,000 tons of coal per year. The population now numbered 500 non-Native people. That year a company backed by British capital bought out the mines and surrounding lands and property from the Hudson's Bay Company and proceeded to expand operations under the name of the Vancouver Coal Mining and Land Company (often shortened to the Vancouver Coal Company). All that remained of the Hudson's Bay Company was a trading post and store.

The new company brought in a locomotive to transport coal from the mines to the docks, where waiting ships carried it to San Francisco. It was Nanaimo coal that fuelled the British navy in the north Pacific, and it was a six-ton lump of Nanaimo coal exhihbited at the World's Fair in London in 1862 that made the little town on Vancouver Island known all over Europe.

The original settlement of Nanaimo grew up around the harbour, where the first coal seams were found on the high ground between the boat basin and Terminal Avenue, which back in those days was a ravine that filled with water at high tide. Gradually the ravine was filled in with material dumped from the mines, and Cameron Island, where upscale condominiums now front the water, became permanently connected to the city shoreline.

*Before the First World War Chinatown flourished along Pine Street and Hecate Street. Fire destroyed many of the buildings in 1960.*

Harbour City *by Paul Grignon captures the tranquil*
*appeal of Newcastle Channel a century ago.*

*The coal mine on Protection Island boasted the deepest*
*shaft in the district, with a slope below Northumberland*
*Channel that ran all the way to Gabriola Island.*

*The Esplanade No. 1 Pit mine on the harbour was the*
*site of a mine explosion that killed 147 in 1887, making*
*it the worst mining accident in B.C.'s history.*

The Vancouver Coal Mining and Land Company decided to plan an organized town and to subdivide and sell lots. The layout of the town was drawn up in England and the lots were sold by auction in Victoria in 1864. The town planners drew a unique blueprint for Nanaimo, with the streets radiating out from the harbour like the spokes of a giant wheel. Many of the streets were named after officials and shareholders of the company. And so, gradually, inhabitants began to build houses up the hill from the harbour and south along the shoreline.

As Nanaimo grew, more land was opened up. Harewood, an area just west of town, had been named for the family of Lieutenant Lascelles, Earl of Harewood, who had invested money in the Harewood mine, which was operated by Robert Dunsmuir. The mine was not a great success, and the land was taken over by the Vancouver Coal Company. Part of it was used for a farm, where the company grew grain for the horses and mules that worked in the mines. The company, under the leadership of Samuel Robins, then divided Harewood into five-acre lots and leased them to the employees with an option to purchase. The area became known as Five Acres, and even today some of these farms are still scattered here and there between the rows of houses. North of town, just over the Millstone River, another residential area was laid out and called Newcastle Townsite.

Now that Nanaimo had a railway, the city almost became a boomtown. But the boom came to an abrupt halt in 1912, when the coal miners went on strike for better working conditions and better treatment. The families of miners walking the picket lines came close to starvation. Those who worked where conditions were good had no interest in walking off the job, and as the strike wore on, tempers ran high.

Even though mining resumed after the strike, and production peaked 10 years later, oil, a much cheaper source of fuel, was already beginning to compete with coal. By the early 1920s California's oil fields were providing 80 percent of the world's energy needs.

In 1874, 400 men were employed in the local mines. That number increased to 2,800 in 1900 and peaked in 1923 at 3,400. By 1947, only 400 men still worked in the mines. By 1955, except for small mining operations carried on by one or two men here and there, the coal-mining industry in Nanaimo had vanished.

Nanaimo produced about 50 million tons of coal in those 100 years. Many lives were lost and many families lived in dire poverty, but it was coal that built the town and created a thriving city. With the loss of its main industry, Nanaimo had a choice: To go the way of other communities that had been founded on a single resource and gradually become a ghost town—a memory, a few pages in the history books—or to reinvent itself and build on the strength of its people, its natural beauty, its glorious harbour, and its other resources.

Nanaimo never had a commercial fishing industry of any note, even though it lies in a sheltered harbour. And even though Nanaimo is situated on a coastal plain that is two to ten miles wide, the soil quality varies tremendously, and most of the land was not arable.

That left logging, but most of the area had been logged off years earlier by small companies. Major sawmills existed in Chemainus and Port Alberni, but never in Nanaimo.

Not surprisingly, as the coal mines closed, Nanaimo's population began to drop. These were tough economic times. By the mid-1930s the population was only slightly more than 6,000 people. The city's only hope was its reputation as a transportation hub. Nanaimo was the closest Island centre to Vancouver, just over two hours away by CPR ferry. From Nanaimo, people and freight could move easily to all points north, west, and south on the Island. Nanaimo's location was a boon to retailers and wholesalers, and they took full advantage of it.

In 1921, 60 percent of the working class was employed in the coal mines. By 1940, 45 percent of working men and women were employed in the service and retail industries. And so Nanaimo began to grow again—slowly and steadily and sometimes with faltering steps.

In 1928 the Malaspina Hotel was built on the waterfront, and in 1940 construction began on the Civic Arena, spearheaded by the Gyro club. The city and the taxpayers supported the project, and four months after ground was broken, the lieutenant-governor of British Columbia, Eric Hamber, declared the arena open.

The Civic Arena was far more than just an artificial skating rink with bleachers, scoreboards, and a sound system—it was a space that would attract shows and conventions and add to the local economy. Indeed, the space was booked up almost immediately for the balance of the year.

Then the Second World War broke out, bringing a boom in manufacturing, but Nanaimo experienced little of that. The men went to war, and 57 gave their lives.

Coal mining did experience a temporary resurgence, and Nanaimo's shipbuilding industry also benefitted. In the first three years, the Newcastle Shipbuilding Company delivered nine hulls to the navy and the air force. At the height of construction, the shipyards employed 158 men.

The postwar years in Nanaimo were lean, but then two things happened that woke up the sleepy little town and gave it a brand new life. The first was Harmac, the pulp mill built in 1948 by H.R. MacMillan, which became Nanaimo's biggest industrial employer.

The second was the election of the new Social Credit Party, with its ambition to make the province a tourist centre. The new government built roads and let the rest of the world know about "Beautiful British Columbia."

Nanaimo boasted of its beauty, and few who came to visit could deny the truth of this. But Nanaimo had something else to offer—a vibrant history, evident everywhere in its downtown streets.

*The old Malaspina Hotel and the post office on Front Street.*

# Samuel Robins

When Samuel Robins became Vancouver Coal Company's mine manager, he put his roots down in the south end—literally and figuratively. A collector of plant specimens from around the world, Robins didn't limit his gardening to his own grounds but planted Lombardy poplars along the Esplanade and Wakesiah Avenue, and poplars, holly trees, and English oaks in Harewood. His sycamore trees curved majestically along Commercial Street. Many of Nanaimo's monkey puzzle trees and Spanish and Chinese chestnuts were planted by him.

Samuel Robins, born in Cornwall, England, on July 7, 1834, came to Nanaimo in 1883. He was thoroughly unimpressed with what he saw and even less so by what he heard. The Vancouver Coal Company was a "stupid old company and the proprietors had more money than brains" according to some. Determined to revitalize the mine, he inspired his workers to give their best. Within five years he had opened new shafts and had equalled the output of the rival Dunsmuir operation.

The miners and townspeople dubbed Robins "The People's Friend". Under his direction the company demonstrated a willingness to co-operate with labour associations, and during his 19 years as superintendent there were no strikes.

Robins saw it as his duty to help the miners achieve the good they had come to Nanaimo to find. He helped workers to own their land and grow their own food. Rental for each lot in the Company's Five Acres development was $2.50 per year for the first two years and $12.50 per year for the next three years, with a purchase price of about $200 per acre. There were some conditions attached. The men had to fence, clear, and cultivate their land. With considerable foresight, Robins wrote into the lease arrangement that the lands were not to be used for trade or any "dangerous" and "noisome" businesses including saloons, pubs, piggeries and slaoughterhouses.

Robins created both the Cricket Field (now Robins Park) and Millstream Park. He provided land for a cemetery, a fire hall, clubhouse, and a rifle range, and he created walking trails through the most beautiful parts of the Company's property, including Newcastle Island.

In 1903 Robins and his wife returned to England, but before they left, Nanaimo held a Sam Robins Day in tribute to his role in the community. Robins died in England on December 30, 1919, at the age of 85. His memory lives on in his magnificent garden on the Esplanade, a street, and the park named in his honour.

*In Harewood, which was called Five Acres during Samuel Robins' time, many of the old farms still produce fruit and crops and the farmhouses are still home to some Nanaimo families.*

# A Walk Through Time

A walk through downtown Nanaimo presents a rare opportunity to step back in time. Self-guided tours are easy, using colourful maps available at the Downtown Nanaimo Partnership office on Commercial Street, the Nanaimo Community Archives on Wharf Street, the Nanaimo District Museum on the hill overlooking the harbour, or at City Hall. Let your imagination run free, and you'll hear the whistle of the old Number 1 mine calling the miners to work, and smell the coal dust in the air. You'll hear the blast of the steam engine chugging into the E & N railway station and the sound of church bells ringing from the tall spires that were once the distinguishing feature of Nanaimo's skyline.

Five distinct Nanaimo walks tell the story of the city's past, shedding light on different historical aspects.

*Above, a backdrop of mountains and classic architecture frame the shoreline parks.*

*Nanaimo is a wonderful place for walkers. The waterfront promenade is Nanaimo's favourite year-round destination for strollers. Other nearby walks include the downtown core, the Old City Quarter, and trails in Bowen Park beside the Millstone River.*

## The Harbour Connection

This walk begins at the Bastion, which overlooks the harbour. This is where it all began. In 1852 Front Street was the heart of Nanaimo. Miners walked to work, so they lived close to the mines. There was a small cluster of cottages within a few hundred feet of the mines, which fronted the harbour. When you walk along Front Street, you can imagine the coal mines that once existed right under your feet.

Along with the miners' cottages, there was a handful of shops and a post office, which probably also functioned as the school and courthouse. These early buildings were designed to be utilitarian, not attractive or even permanent. After all, when the coal seams were exhausted, the men would move on.

If you stand in Pioneer Plaza just beside the Bastion and look out over the harbour, you will see almost exactly what the early miners looked at every morning as they went to work—except for the pretty sailboats dotting the water and the floatplanes lifting into the sky with a great roar of engines. There is Protection Island with its tall cedars and firs, Newcastle Island with its rocky shoreline, and the safe, sheltered harbour.

But if you turn to look inland, you will have to strain your imagination to see what those miners saw. The change in structure is dramatic, but not nearly as startling as the change in the land itself. Many of the main streets were channels of water. Cameron Island, with its modern apartment buildings, was truly an island cut off from the rest of Nanaimo. The lower part of Front Street, where the Port Theatre sits, was under water, and Terminal Avenue, the main highway running through town, was a water-filled ravine.

The entire waterfront has changed, and even the Bastion, the oldest building in Nanaimo, is not in its original location, a site across the street. When the property was sold in 1891, the Bastion was moved in what was probably the province's first preservation effort. Then in the early 1970s, when Front Street was widened, the Bastion was moved again, slightly south and east to its present location. The Bastion exemplifies Nanaimo's early architecture: It is rough, wooden, and highly practical.

As you walk north on Front Street, you will come upon the courthouse, which was Nanaimo's first city hall and was built of stone between 1895 and 1896. The architect, Francis Mawson Rattenbury, was a colourful and notorious character. He emigrated from England in 1892 at the age of 26 and won the competition to design the provincial Legislative Buildings in Victoria, much to the chagrin of older and more established professionals. Like those buildings, the courthouse is solid, permanent, and grand in its Richardsonian Romanesque style of architecture. It features rough-dressed ashlar masonry and prominent arched openings typical of this style. It is massive and authoritative, and to further enhance the building's presence, Rattenbury set it to the rear of the sloping site, allowing for a

*The historic Nanaimo Courthouse, built by noted architect Francis Rattenbury, is a distinguished Nanaimo landmark.*

*Beside Dallas Square, St. Paul's Anglican Church (on the right behind the bandstand) held its opening service June 8, 1862. Note the Bastion on the left.*

gracious, landscaped plaza at the front. This imposing building heralded a shift from pioneer culture and made the proud statement that Nanaimo was here to stay.

Past the courthouse is the Globe Hotel, which was constructed in 1887. Its most unusual feature is a mansard roof, the only one in the city. The Globe, like the courthouse, presents a grand and elegant face to the street.

Georgia Park, its entrance marked by totem poles and a historic canoe, has been part of Nanaimo for many years. This was the park where people gathered with picnic lunches and watched boat races in the harbour below—but the water was much closer to the park then. Swy-A-Lana Lagoon and Maffeo Sutton Park are entirely man-made.

Walking down the hill and around the corner you'll come upon the Nanaimo Foundry. Constructed in 1913, the Foundry made equipment and machinery for Nanaimo and surrounding areas and is Nanaimo's last good remaining example of the city's early industrial development.

The Civic Arena, just to the front of Swy-A-Lana Lagoon and next to the Foundry, was built in 1941 and was Nanaimo's social centre. Today it's a skating rink, but back then it was used for meetings, conventions, social programs, and all sorts of entertainment.

Coming back up the hill and walking back on Front Street, take a look at some of the buildings and imagine what they may have been used for in the past. True, many have been significantly renovated, but when you learn that Front Street was Nanaimo's early "automobile row," you will see the evidence all around you. One auto body shop is still in operation and once, years ago, when they changed signs on the front of the building, they discovered the outline of the old Texaco star still etched in the weathered concrete. From the early 1920s until the 1960s this was the "strip." If you look closely at the bistro near the corner of Church Street, you'll recognize the typical square shape of a gas station, and you may even be able to locate where the gas pumps used to be.

The harbour today is Nanaimo's favourite walking place, with parks, gardens, and charming boutiques. In Nanaimo's past it was a working harbour lined with wharves, and was named a port of entry in 1863. A merchant named John Hirst

built a stone warehouse on the waterfront that is now part of the Port Authority's offices. Below the warehouse was Hirst's wharf, one of many that jutted out into the harbour to accommodate ships from all over the world. It was here that new immigrants landed and coal was loaded onto giant freighters. Today ships still dock here, and they still bring people, but now the people are usually American and the ships are pocket (small) cruise ships bound for Alaska's fjords.

*The Festival of Banners is an annual exposition that features colourful banners gracing the streets of downtown Nanaimo and decorating the waterfront walkway.*

*The boat basin in Nanaimo's harbour was once a mass of commercial warehouses and dock facilities for cargo boats and passenger vessels alike.*

*Nanaimo's waterfront walkway winds along the downtown harbour and out to the charming Swy-A-Lana Lagoon, a favourite Nanaimo park.*

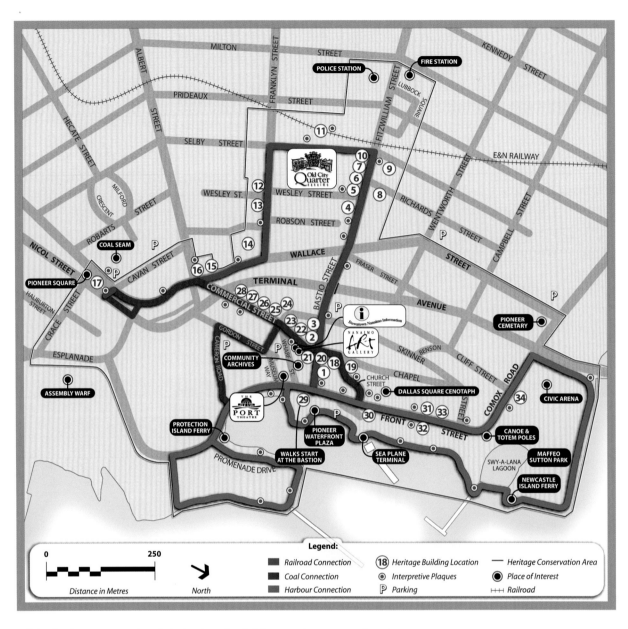

*Of the five heritage areas described, the three detailed here are the most popular. City brochures on all walks are available at the Information Centre or through the city web site at www.city.nanaimo.ca. (Map courtesy of the Nanaimo Community Heritage Commission.)*

## The Railroad Connection

Fitzwilliam Street was difficult to reach before the bridge was built across the ravine in 1875, making it easier for the Presbyterians and the Roman Catholics to get to church. Then the Sisters of St. Ann built a convent on the rocky bluff across the street, where they nursed the sick and schooled children of all creeds.

The completion of the Esquimalt and Nanaimo Railway in 1886 resulted in saloons, restaurants, and hotels being built along Fitzwilliam Street. The railway gave a boost to the local economy by bringing in special tourist excursions, but later reversed the impact by offering free trips to Victoria for trainloads of shoppers.

After the turn of the century, a number of wood-frame commercial buildings were built close to the station, and though railway traffic isn't as important as it used to be, those old buildings have been revitalized and house thriving businesses to this day.

1. B.C. Telephone Exchange, 70-76 Bastion St.
2. Commercial Hotel, 121 Bastion St.
3. Eagle's Hall, 133-141 Bastion St.
4. St. Andrew's United Church, 315 Fitzwilliam St.
5. S&W Apartments, 403-409 Fitzwilliam St.
6. Mitchell's Market, 411 Fitzwilliam St.
7. T&B Apartments, 413 - 417 Fitzwilliam St.
8. Angell's Trading, 426 Fitzwilliam St.
9. Occidental Hotel, 432 Fitzwilliam St.
10. Rawlinson & Glaholm Grocers, 437 Fitzwilliam St.
11. Esquimalt & Nanaimo Railway Station, 321 Selby St.
12. Franklyn Street Gymnasium, 421 Franklyn St.
13. Harris Residence, 375 Franklyn St.
14. Nanaimo City Hall, 455 Wallace St.
15. Brumpton Block, 481-489 Wallace St.
16. Merchant's Bank of Canada, 499 Wallace St.
17. Nanaimo Fire Hall #2, 34 Nicol St.

## The Coal Connection

Commercial Street began as a trail that followed the contours of Commercial Inlet to the mine sites and miners' cottages.

Most of the buildings on the water side sat on pilings and were destroyed in the fire of 1878. Some were rebuilt, only to be destroyed by another fire in 1894.

By then, the shipping of coal had moved away from the downtown area, but the coal connection was maintained when the Vancouver Coal Company started to reclaim the tidal inlets. Today all that remains of the coal connection is a distant memory of depression-era miners running through town to work, their hobnailed boots striking sparks on the road in the early morning darkness.

18. The Earl Block, 2-4 Church St.
19. The Great National Land Building, 5-17 Church St.
20. The Halse Block, 200-206 Commercial St.
21. A.R. Johnston & Co. Grocers, 172-174 Commercial St.
22. The Parkin Block, 143-155 Commercial St.
23. Ashlar Lodge Masonic Temple, 101 Commercial St.
24. The Hirst Block, 93-99 Commercial St.
25. The Rogers Block, 83-87 Commercial St.
26. The Hall Block, 37-45 Commercial St.
27. Nash Hardware, 19 Commercial St.
28. Nanaimo-Duncan Utilities Building, 13 Commercial St.

## The Harbour Connection

The City of Nanaimo began on Front Street after the discovery of coal attracted the Hudson's Bay Company to the area. It was just below the HBC's bastion that the first mining families stepped ashore in 1854 after their six-month-long voyage around Cape Horn on the *Princess Royal*. They were greeted by Scottish miners and housed in log cabins along Front Street.

The harbour was declared a port of entry in 1863. John Hirst built a stone warehouse, and his wharf was one of many that jutted out into the harbour to accommodate ships from all over the world.

Front Street leads to Comox Road and the Pioneer Cemetery, the final resting place for thousands of immigrants who came by ship to Nanaimo in the years since 1852. People still come by the harbour connection, not by barque or collier anymore, but by float plane, ferry, yacht, and freighter.

29. The Bastion, 98 Front St.
30. Post Office and Federal Building, 54-66 Front St.
31. Nanaimo Court House, 31-35 Front St.
32. Tom Brown's Auto Body, 28 Front St.
33. Globe Hotel, 25 Front St.
34. Nanaimo Foundry, 4 - 100 Comox Rd.

## The Coal Connection

Start your tour of Nanaimo's coal history on the corner of Front and Church streets, where an enormous lump of black coal commemorates "100 Years of Coal." Church Street curves around to join Commercial Street, which continues to flow gracefully down to Terminal Avenue.

There are many significant buildings worthy of note in Nanaimo's downtown core. Perhaps the most impressive is the Great National Land Building at 17 Church Street, which was constructed in 1914. The beautiful curving columns and the graceful sweep of the face of the building are, however, not unique. The building was originally a Bank of Commerce and the plans were standard for many banks throughout the country. In fact, there are duplicates still standing in other parts of Canada.

The Earl Block at 24 Church Street was built around 1888 and is a proud surviving example of a brick-faced commercial building of the Victorian era. The Halse Block and the old A.R. Johnson & Co. Grocer at 172 Commercial Street are excellent examples of Edwardian architecture, while the Parkin Block exemplifies the type of building erected after the First World War. The Ashlar Lodge was built in 1923 on the site of an earlier Masonic Temple, the first in B.C. It continues to be used for by the Freemasons today.

Commercial Street began as a trail that followed the contours of Commercial Inlet and meandered past the mines and miners' cottages. Here you will see Nanaimo's greatest concentration of heritage buildings. As you walk down Commercial Street, you will notice a distinct difference between the east and west sides of the street. On the west side

*Ships and industry have always been big contributors to the vitality of the harbour.*

# Che-wech-i-kan

History books say that it was a Snuneymuxw man who sealed his village's fate with the discovery of "black diamonds." In 1851 Che-wech-i-kan was trading his pelts at the Hudson's Bay Company fort in Victoria, and he visited the blacksmith's shop. As he watched the smith working at the forge, firing it with coal, he asked where the coal had come from.

It was shipped across the ocean from England, the smith told him, and because it had travelled such a long distance it was very valuable—more valuable than fur.

Che-wech-i-kan was not impressed. He could get plenty of that, he said. He found great lumps of it when he dug for clams, and often used it instead of wood. Che-wech-i-kan's words eventually reached the ears of Joseph MacKay, the clerk at the post, who promised a substantial reward for proof.

The next summer Che-wech-i-kan came back to the fort with a load of coal stashed in the bottom of his canoe. It was the real thing, all right, and what's

more, the quality was excellent. MacKay immediately reported the find to James Douglas, the Chief Factor of the Hudson's Bay Company at Victoria, who sent him to investigate. Che-wech-i-kan was generously rewarded for his find and was given the name "Coal Tyee" or "Coal Chief."

you can almost go back in time. Very little has changed here. The architecture, particularly in the ornate detailing around the rooflines, has the feel of a charming, Edwardian-era town. But look across the street and you'll see far more cement and far less ornamentation. The explanation is intriguing.

The buildings on the east, or water, side of Commercial Street were built on pilings along the shoreline, literally above the water. One Nanaimo resident whose father owned a shop on Commercial Street recalls that they used to tie their rowboat up at the back door. But gradually Commercial Inlet was filled

in, and the owners eventually took the buildings off their stilts and settled them on new foundations. Most of them also updated the buildings with new stucco or siding, and much of the old ornamentation disappeared in favour of the modern, streamlined look of the 1950s and 1960s. The buildings across the street didn't need to be shifted, so their owners saved themselves the time and expense of changing anything at all.

The Hall Block, at 37–45 Commercial Street, was constructed in 1925 by Dr. G.A.B. Hall, who was also Nanaimo's mayor in 1930 and 1931. At the corner of Commercial Street

*Earl Block was built around 1888 and is an excellent example of the brick-faced commercial buildings of downtown Nanaimo's Victorian era.*

and Terminal Avenue stands the old Nanaimo–Duncan Utilities building, erected in 1941 and a fine example of the art-deco style of architecture. With its unique triangular shape, it also makes excellent use of its corner location.

At the end of Commercial Street, you cross Terminal Avenue and continue your walk along Victoria Crescent. Some of the buildings here are even older than those on the north side of Terminal. Many of them are faced with the typical 1870s "boomtown" false front. Keep going along Victoria Crescent, and at the corner of Victoria Street and Cavan, what looks like an ordinary cliff is perhaps Nanaimo's most poignant reminder of its early history. The cliff is a coal seam that was part of the Park Head mine and is virtually the only place in Nanaimo where you can see and touch the black diamonds that brought the early settlers.

Directly across the street from the coal seam is the old fire hall, which was built to replace the first fire hall—destroyed, ironically, by fire in 1894. Originally there was a 60-foot-high

brick hose tower at the front of the building. In 1914 a concrete tower was added to the rear. The big doors at the front were the exit for the horses pulling the fire carts.

*Nanaimo's Great National Land Building is a historic landmark and one of Nanaimo's architectural treasures.*

34

*Nanaimo's old fire hall No.2, now housing a popular upscale restaurant, was constructed in 1893 to replace the first fire hall, which burned down.*

*Most of these Commercial Street buildings from the 1950s are largely unchanged today. Nanaimo has done an excellent job of preserving its heritage structures.*

## The Railroad Connection

Fitzwilliam Street, named after a chairman of the Vancouver Coal Company, wasn't much of a street until the bridge that connects it to downtown was built across Terminal Avenue. And even then, it wasn't until the Esquimalt and Nanaimo Railway arrived in 1886 that Fitzwilliam really blossomed. New restaurants and hotels sprang up to entertain visitors arriving by train. Today, the railway station is seldom used. Twice a day the Dayliner stops on its way to or from Victoria, and after a brief bustle, silence falls back on the old building. But the wooden buildings that were erected on Fitzwilliam Street are still thriving as chic little boutiques and restaurants in an area known as the Old City Quarter.

The Occidental Hotel still stands on the corner of Fitzwilliam and Selby streets and still dispenses beer on tap. St. Andrew's United Church, which was Presbyterian when it was built in 1893, is virtually unchanged, with its picturesque roofline and tall bell tower. All up and down Fitzwilliam Street are charming stores that were once hotels, and above some of these shops are Nanaimo's first residential apartments. Some of these apartments now house offices, but many are still used as residences.

*The E & N Dayliner still stops at the historic railway station near Nanaimo's Old City Quarter.*

# Robert Dunsmuir

In 1869 Robert Dunsmuir, who had come to Vancouver Island to work as a miner for the Hudson's Bay Company, discovered coal at Wellington, just east of Harewood. From then on, there were two main coal-mining operations in Nanaimo: The Vancouver Coal Mining and Land Company, which had expanded its operation to include Newcastle Island, and the Robert Dunsmuir and Sons mine.

Robert Dunsmuir had a reputation as a mine owner with an iron hand and heel. In 1877 Dunsmuir heard that the men were talking about going on strike. Their salaries ranged from $2.50 to $5 per day, and they wanted more money. Before they could mount a strike, Dunsmuir locked them out. Then Dunsmuir appealed to his friends in the government in Victoria, which obligingly sent police and soldiers to Nanaimo to cause as much trouble as possible for the miners. After four months, the miners' spirits were broken. Desperate to earn money, they agreed to go back to work at a maximum wage of $2.50 per day.

In 1883 Robert Dunsmuir pulled off his biggest coup. He had a dream of joining Nanaimo to Victoria by rail, and so he proposed to build the Esquimalt & Nanaimo Railway. Dunsmuir raised half the capital from American investors, and in return for building his dream, the Canadian government awarded him a $750,000 cash subsidy and 2 million acres of land, including mineral rights. Dunsmuir was literally given one-fifth of Vancouver Island. In August 1886 after Prime Minister John A. Macdonald drove the last spike he, Robert Dunsmuir and their wives came by special train to Nanaimo, where they were greeted by 17 blasts from the Bastion cannons.

Perhaps the most interesting thing about this area is the residential neighbourhood surrounding the commercial buildings. This is an attractive and unique part of historic Nanaimo; some of the city's most beautiful homes were built here or on Stewart Avenue. The higher up the hill you go on Fitzwilliam Street, the grander the homes—and the more panoramic the views. Some of the larger houses have now been turned into apartments, although many have been meticulously restored as family homes.

Even as late as the early 20th century, you could stand at the top of Fitzwilliam Street and gaze down on a skyscape punctuated by the spires of St. Peter's, St Paul's, the Wallace Street Methodist Church, and both St. Andrew's churches. On Sunday mornings the town echoed with the pealing of bells. Only two of those churches remain, the others having been demolished to make way for new government and office buildings.

## The South End

Nanaimo's south end, although not nearly as prominent an area as downtown or the Old City Quarter, is one of the city's most historically significant and retains many interesting if unassuming facets.

The south end started in the shadows of the No. 1 mine, the first area of homes built up by miners, storekeepers, and mine executives. Today many of the original homes are still standing, little changed from 150 years ago, in a neighbourhood that still has much of the feel of a mining town. Gillespie Street seems a place that time forgot. It is easy to imagine an unpaved, muddy, rutted road, with an old nag tied to a post and a barrow leaning up against the fence. The miners' two- or three-room cottages are set close to the road, many featuring an altered roof line where upper rooms have been added at a later date.

Some of the south end's industrial past also remains. A mine rescue station on Farquhar Street, built in 1913, is virtually intact. Nanaimo's coal mines were among the most dangerous in the world—more than 2,000 miners were killed or injured by explosions, falling rocks and coal, drowning, and carelessly tended equipment. In the event of an emergency, rescue teams would crawl into the mines to bring out the dead and the survivors. Today the old rescue station houses a neighbourhood drop-in centre.

Haliburton Street was lined with hotels and stores, the south end's equivalent of Commercial Street. Early mine managers built their gingerbread-embellished homes here too. Some still stand.

At the corner of Esplanade and Fry streets grows a most remarkable garden. It is not what you might traditionally think of as a garden. There are no groves of brilliant rhododendrons, no rose bushes, no charming Japanese ponds, or colourful beds of marigolds and petunias. This garden covers an entire city block and looms above a cluster of derelict cottages whose unkempt lawns are choked with weeds. But towering overhead is a canopy of treetops reaching high into the sky. The Blue Atlas Cedar and a giant sequoia give shade to a black mulberry tree and Nanaimo's only evergreen oak tree. These rare and beautiful specimens were planted by Samuel Matthew Robins, the superintendent of the Vancouver Coal Company, between 1884 and 1903.

Robins asked visiting sea captains to bring him samples of trees either from their home countries or from their ports of call, and with these seedlings he created a small Eden that still survives.

Among the humble cottages and elaborate homes of the south end sits a simple plaque at 1151 Milton Street, the site where the Vancouver Coal Company opened the Number 1 Esplanade mine in 1883. The plaque, which notes that the mine produced 18 million tons of coal by the time it was closed in 1938, pays tribute to the 153 miners who lost their lives in an 1887 mine explosion.

## The Newcastle Neighbourhood

When coal mining reached its peak in Nanaimo in the early 1900s, the south end, where many of the wealthier people lived, became highly industrialized. Those who could afford to leave the neighbourhood for quieter and more genteel surroundings did so. Many of them moved north across the bridge that crosses the Millstone River and built grand homes along Stewart Avenue, the broad street that leads today to the Departure Bay ferry terminal, and along Vancouver Avenue just up the hill behind Stewart.

This neighbourhood was called Newcastle, after Newcastle Island, which was the most prominent sight from every property in the area. Newcastle is bounded on the north by Townsite Road and on the south by the Millstone River. It is a compact neighbourhood, but it features some of the most beautiful and historically significant homes in Nanaimo.

*Some of Nanaimo's most beautiful heritage homes are located in the Old City Quarter and in the Newcastle neighbourhood.*

*Opposite: Vancouver Coal Mining and Land Company's Shaft No. 1 at Nanaimo in 1884. Three years later it was the scene of a horrible mine disaster.*

This was the first neighbourhood where the notion of zoning came into play and the first that was strictly residential. When the great mansions were being built, Newcastle was considered a suburb. The grand homes of that era were demolished during the 1920s and '30s and replaced with charming Craftsman-style buildings, but traces of the manors still remain. At the corner of Stewart Avenue and Bryden Street, for instance, stands a pair of massive gateposts and a wrought-iron gate that marked the entry to Eldovilla, the estate built by William Sloan, who made the second-largest recorded fortune in the Klondike gold rush.

The Newcastle neighbourhood contains homes like the Johnston residence, built in 1912 and considered a superior example of the Craftsman style, with features like a complex gable roof and an unusual round projecting bay at the northwest corner. The Van Houton residence, with its open front verandah, and the Sharp residence, with its innovative use of brick, are two other excellent examples of that era's Craftsman construction.

Perhaps the best-known landmark in the neighbourhood is the old Hoggan's Store at 404 Stewart Avenue. One of the first neighbourhood stores in the city, it was built in 1914 entirely of brick and featured a wharf at the rear where fishermen could dock and load up on supplies.

Not surprisingly, the site selected for the Nanaimo Yacht Club in 1909 was at the foot of Rosehill Street, one block south of Stewart Avenue. Only the wealthier members of the community could afford pleasure boats and participate in races through the Gulf and San Juan islands. The Yacht Club was exclusive in the early days, and the clubhouse was the focal point of many social occasions. Today the Nanaimo Yacht Club is still a hub for boaters and sailors, although membership is far less exclusive.

# Nanaimo Today: "The Harbour City"

With the introduction of regular ferry service from the mainland, Nanaimo became known as the transportation hub for Vancouver Island. Even today with BC Ferries, the *Harbour Lynx* catamaran, three air services to the harbour, and an excellent peripheral highway system, Nanaimo is the mid-Island's main trading centre. While this led some pundits to dub it as the "hub city," the city's residents have always known that the focal point is the waterfront. It has changed dramatically since the Spanish explorers first admired the sheltered waters, but the setting is still one of the most beautiful in the world. Today the steady bustle of sailboats, planes, ferries, and working vessels has earned it the simple moniker "The Harbour City."

The Nanaimo Port Authority worked for years to create an attractive waterfront walkway that winds around pretty parks and the sheltered Swy-A-Lana Lagoon. It hugs the seaside past the Nanaimo Yacht Club and leads to the terminus for the Vancouver ferries at Departure Bay.

In the harbour, the masts of fishing boats rise like a forest of trees along the docks. At the fish market pier, you can purchase fresh salmon, prawns, snapper, and other "catches of the day."

*The Friday Farmer's Market in Pioneer Plaza doesn't just offer up fresh produce and local crafts. On most days local talent entertains the shoppers and those who just like to soak up the sounds and atmosphere of the waterfront.*

In summer, the Bastion's cannon booms across the harbour at noon. Across the street sits the award-winning 800-seat Port Theatre, home of the Vancouver Island Symphony and host to professional and community productions year-round.

You can stroll south along the Harbourside Walkway past the wharfinger's office and down to the wharves themselves, where the Protection Island ferry plies its way back and forth every hour, carrying hundreds of tourists and locals to the floating Dinghy Dock Pub during the summer months. You may find that this section of the walkway, which skirts the fishing-boat piers, has the most charm—the smell of the sea, the sight of fishermen cleaning their nets and gear, the tall masts swaying gently with the rise and fall of the water, and the high-pitched cry of the seagulls all conspire to create a romantic mood.

The walkway takes you to man-made Cameron Island, past the exclusive condominiums, and to the Visiting Vessel Pier where pocket cruise ships tie up. It is also from here that the annual Cadillac Van Isle 360° International Yacht Race, which circumnavigates Vancouver Island, sets off. The walkway then curves around Cameron Island and ends at the ferry dock from which the car ferry shuttles passengers back and forth between Nanaimo and Gabriola Island, well known for its artists and artisans.

West of the harbour are Nanaimo's busy downtown and the Old City Quarter rising up the hill, where the view of sailboats, cruise ships, float planes, ferries, and cargo ships in the bay bear witness to the city's name: The Harbour City.

The Harbour Lynx *catamaran is the latest transportation link to
Vancouver, covering downtown to downtown in 75 minutes.*

*The thriving harbour is home to an active seaplane terminal
and colourful commercial float as well as numerous shops.*

*Nanaimo's waterfront is the perfect place to stop at a floating restaurant and dig into really fresh fish 'n chips.*

*Near the span that crosses Swy-A-Lana Lagoon strollers may continue their walk from downtown to the Millstone River or use this tidal ramp to reach a floating fishing pier that is popular with young and old alike.*

*Visitors are always thrilled to watch (and hear) the Bastion's old cannon explode with sound. Here, piper Bill Poppy adds to the festivity of the occasion on the upper level of Pioneer Plaza.*

*Nanaimo is a boater's paradise. It doesn't mater if you are paddling a kayak or sailing a catamaran, you'll find adventure in Nanaimo's waters.*

# The Arts

The West Coast, with its easy lifestyle, mild climate, and majestic scenery, has been attracting artists since settlers first came to these shores. Nanaimo has a particularly rich and lively arts scene based downtown. The arts community welcomes artisans, writers, poets, painters, and musicians with unalloyed enthusiasm. Nanaimo has earned a reputation as a breeding ground for jazz musicians and is the home of such international jazz stars as Diana Krall and Ingrid Jensen. The city's jazz program in schools is well known for its calibre.

Nanaimo's CIBC Centre for the Arts at 150 Commercial Street is home to the downtown Nanaimo Art Gallery. Shows change monthly and concentrate on the area's top artists, such as Grant Leier, Nixie Barton, Fred Peters, and Jan Smart. Bring the kids and they'll discover their own "hands-on" display where they can create art with dozens of bits and pieces of creative material.

The Centre for the Arts is also home to Film Nanaimo, Theatre BC, Dance on the Crimson Coast Society, the Vancouver Island Symphony, and the Nanaimo Community Archives.

*Gallery 223 (above) at 223 Commercial Street is one of many fine galleries in the downtown Arts District.* Iron Man *by Mike Szucs is the enigmatic giant that welcomes visitors to the Art Gallery at Malaspina University-College.*

Nanaimo boasts excellent community theatre groups as well as two professional theatre companies. The Nanaimo Concert Band, the Malaspina Choir, A Cappella Plus, and the Bel Canto singers all make Nanaimo their home. The Port Theatre brings in national and international productions year-round. Within one year of opening its doors, the Port Theatre was nominated in its category at the Canadian Music Week Convention as one of the best theatres in Canada.

Book launches are almost a weekly event in Nanaimo as the city's many hometown authors and other Canadian and international writers visit local booksellers. Nanaimo is home to potters, weavers, doll makers, and award-winning woodworkers. The city is also the site of one of only three Tozan wood-fired kilns in the world.

There is an almost overwhelming resource of artists in Nanaimo in every field. These artists have come to Nanaimo from many parts of the world, each bringing his or her own creativity and style. When Nanaimo became a haven for artists, there was no master plan. The result is an eclectic group of people whose delight in their work shines in dozens of venues all over the city.

*Pioneer Plaza with its elegant shops, charming cafés, fisherman's pier, and walkway is one of the hubs of downtown activity. Regular seaplane service and the* Harbour Lynx *catamaran make day trips from Vancouver convenient.*

Children are inspired and encouraged to participate in Nanaimo's arts community.

The annual International Festival attracts children and their families from all over Vancouver Island and helps Nanaimo celebrate its artistic community.

Nanaimo boasts a vibrant art scene, which centres in the historic downtown Arts District.

# Festivals and Special Events

It is quite possible that no other city in Canada has as many annual festivals and events as does the Harbour City. The Francophone Maple Sugar Festival, Festival of Banners, Children's Book Festival, Vancouver Island International Festival, Empire Days, Cadillac Van Isle 360 International Yacht Race, a leg of the Motocross Pro-National Championship Race, Dragon Boat Festival, Silly Boat Regatta, Marine Festival (which culminates in a fabulous fireworks display and the World Championship Bathtub Race), Symphony in the Harbour, Vancouver Island Exhibition, Cans Food Festival, Adventure Games, Infringing Dance Festival, inFEST Film Festival, Wine Festival, the post-Halloween pumpkin display along Jingle Pot Road's "Shady Mile", and the Festival of Trees all take place in Nanaimo each year.

## Winter/Spring Festivals

The celebration begins in mid-February with the four-day **Maple Sugar Festival** staged by Nanaimo's Francophone Society. Schoolchildren arrive in busloads at the Beban Park recreational complex to taste maple sugar, learn about its manufacture, enjoy French entertainers, and try their hand at maple sugaring in the snow. The festival spreads to the heart of downtown Nanaimo, where ice carvers demonstrate their craft and musicians entertain the crowds in the Harbourfront Plaza.

*The annual Maple Sugar Festival is a delight for everyone and introduces Francophone culture to Nanaimo children.*

*Opposite: Jugglers of varying sizes entertain during the Vancouver Island International Festival.*

*The Vancouver Island International Festival brings the world's best children's entertainment to town. Library Square and other open-air venues host performers. The Port Theatre (left) is the venue for some of the most spectacular main stage acts.*

Nanaimo's **Festival of Banners** is an original art exposition that has enthralled many visitors, some of whom have taken the idea back to their own communities. Each year in early spring, adults and children design and paint the hundreds of banners that grace the city streets and create a festival atmosphere all summer long. The annual hanging of the banners in early May is the city's signal that summer has officially begun.

The annual **Children's Book Festival** at Malaspina University-College in early May brings internationally acclaimed children's authors to town. During this one-day fair, children meet their favourite authors, listen to stories, and walk away proudly clutching autographed copies of their favourite books.

In mid-May the **Vancouver Island International Festival** takes over the Port Theatre and the downtown core with children's entertainment from around the world. Up to 10,000 children arrive in Nanaimo from as far away as Victoria and Port Hardy to be entertained by internationally acclaimed acts from Africa, Australia, Denmark, Canada, Brazil, Mexico, and other parts of the world.

**Empire Days** celebrates Queen Victoria's birthday during the May long weekend and is one of Nanaimo's most cherished and long-standing traditions. The event features a grand parade through the downtown streets, a royal tea, and the crowning of the May Queen and her attendants, who are children chosen from a different elementary school each year.

HMCS Oriole *vies for position amongst the faster, lighter craft anxious to pass the harbour's starting line.*

## The Nautical Festivals

In early June more than 30 racing yachts take over the harbour for the start of the **Cadillac Van Isle 360 International Yacht Race**, which circumnavigates Vancouver Island in 10 legs and covers a distance of 580 nautical mules. Participants sail counter-clockwise with stops at French Creek, Comox, Campbell River, Hardwicke Island, Telegraph Cove, Port Hardy, Winter Harbour, Ucluelet and Victoria before returning to the Nanaimo finish line.

In the the inaugural 2000 race, the fleet encountered a sensational storm near Winter Harbour at the northwest tip of the Island that took out sails and masts and convinced more than one participant to drop out. The racers experienced a sense of camaraderie and sportsmanship that is rare in the world of international yacht racing. At the end of the race, one boater summed up the event: "The race changes strangers into friends and friends into family—a family known as the fleet of the Cadillac Van Isle 360."

In 2004 July became Marine Festival month when the three-weekend sequence of water races got started with an emotion-filled two days of dragon boat racing. Nanaimo's first **Dragon Boat Festival** took place in early July 2003. More than 30 teams of paddlers raced in the waters off Maffeo Sutton Park in their long canoes. A highlight of the event was the moving ceremony called "Waking the Dragon," in which a Taoist priest blessed the boats the evening before the race. Thousands came to watch and take part in the rich eastern traditions and festivities during the three days of the race, ensuring its success as an annual event.

*On Canada Day thousands throng the waterfront to take in the spectacular fireworks display. July also marks the beginning of Marine Festival month in Nanaimo when all eyes again turn to the harbour.*

*Based at Esquimalt, the historic HMCS Oriole, a 102-foot navy sailing ship is a frequent visitor to Nanaimo's harbour and a participant in the annual Van Isle 360 Yacht Race.*

*Each year the Cadillac Van Isle 360 Yacht Race sets out on its 10-leg odyssey from Nanaimo's harbour to circumnavigate Vancouver Island. At left, the fleet jockeys for position as the race nears its beginning. Upper right, the crew of the* Hard Drive, *a 38-3 C&C out of Maple Bay, begins 10 days of hard sailing en route to a seventh-place finish.*

*Racers go all out in groups of four dragon-boat crews totally dedicated to reaching the finish line first.*

In 2004, the highlight was the Breast Cancer Survivors Carnation Ceremony when eight dragon boats with teams made up of women who had overcome cancer paid tribute to the less fortunate. Their salute of pink carnations was accompanied by festive music and the shoreline cheers of thousands.

Each year in mid-July, Swy-A-Lana Lagoon is overrun by hundreds of rather silly people armed with water cannons, duct tape, elastic bands, rubber floats, hammers, nails, and a truly bizarre selection of costumes. The aim of the **Silly Boat Regatta** is to propel a built-on-site craft out to a turnaround point in Swy-A-Lana Lagoon and back in the shortest time. But everyone who has ever watched or taken part in the race knows the real goal is to stay afloat. Water bombing the opposition is all in the name of fair play and is highly encouraged. Nanaimo's Child Development Centre is the beneficiary of the entire fundraising scheme.

Following the Silly Boat Regatta in July is Nanaimo's grandest and most famous celebration, the original Marine Festival. People have long associated the Marine Festival with the World Championship Bathtub Race and the spectacular fireworks display on the evening of the last day, but the festival takes place over four days, and the entire town turns out to party. Downtown's Commercial Street becomes the venue for live bands, dancing, clowns, land bathtub races, bubble-gum-blowing contests, waiters' races, and other activities. It's Nanaimo's version of Mardi Gras, and it's pure family fun.

*Nanaimo's harbour is the setting for the annual Dragon Boat Festival — a stirring and emotional event that is as exciting for spectators as it is for the competitors. Up to 40 teams compete with the Breast Cancer Survivor teams.*

*The silly-boat construction zone brings howls of laughter and strokes of ingenuity to the
fore — good times for all. Every year more and more entrants add to the festivities.*

*Thousands of people gather at Swy-a-Lana Lagoon every summer to participate in the Silly Boat Regatta and to
cheer on their favourite team. It isn't whether you win or lose — it's whether or not your boat stays afloat.*

Hundreds of tubbers take to the waters off Nanaimo during the annual Marine Festival to compete in the World Championship Bathtub Race. The race now starts in Nanaimo's harbour and ends in Departure Bay, but in 1967 when it started and for many years thereafter, tubbers crossed Georgia Strait to finish the race in Vancouver.

A giant bathtub carries race officials who enjoy a perfect vantage point for the action. The "big tub" is a familiar sight in Nanaimo and is always a popular parade entry. The racecourse has tubbers setting a WNW course to Schooner Cove before they return to Departure Bay.

## The Bathtub Race

Nanaimo's **World Championship Bathtub Race** may have an odd-sounding name, but it's a deadly serious sport involving small fibreglass hulls outfitted with powerful engines that take racers on a deliriously fast and bone-jarring ride that departs Nanaimo Harbour, rounds Entrance Island, and circles the Winchelsea Islands north of the city. Racers then roar south, hugging the shoreline to land at Departure Bay beach. But landing the tubs isn't the end of the race. From there, exhausted tubbers unwind their cramped legs and sprint (or hobble) up the beach to ring the victory bell. The tubbers sometimes have to battle rough seas and drenching rain, but in calm conditions the winners can complete the 36 kilometres in about an hour.

Participants in the very first bathtub race probably wouldn't recognize today's version as the same event. The inaugural World Championship Bathtub Race from Nanaimo to Kitsilano Beach in Vancouver took place in 1967 as a publicity stunt dreamed up by Mayor Frank Ney and local realtor Glenn Galloway. That first year, everyone thought it was a lark. Since there weren't any rules to speak of, other than that the vessel had to be a bathtub, would-be racers put together anything they thought might float.

Firemen tied together a bunch of gallon drums, put a platform on top, and stuck a pole on it from which they flew a pair of red long johns stuffed with balloons. They had a crank-up air horn on board, a fire hydrant with a plastic dog attached to it, and, of course, a bathtub. It took the firemen three hours and 45 gallons of gas to get as far as Entrance Island.

The United States Navy entered a bathtub that looked pretty ordinary until it got up to speed and emerged from the waves on three stilt-like projections. The driver stood in the tub sporting an impressive gold-braided hat. Then he hit a wave and sank, valiantly going down with the boat until only his hat was left floating on the waves.

The Pacific Biological Station built an entire bathroom on a raft, including a toilet, tub, and shower and named it "Strait Flush."

Race organizers didn't expect anyone to actually finish the race, and when one entrant did, they were so amazed they didn't quite know what to do about it.

Within a few years of the first race, people began to take tubbing seriously. They never forgot to have fun, but they were determined to cross the Strait of Georgia and be the first to land on the sand at Kitsilano.

A giant tub was built to ferry around race officials, and Frank Ney was always there in the thick of it, wearing his pirate's costume, brandishing his sword, and urging the racers to victory.

The race has changed, but fun will always play a big part. Now that the race leaves Nanaimo from the harbour and ends at Departure Bay, Nanaimo residents can watch the beginning and the end and be there to cheer the winner on as he makes his way up the beach to ring the bell.

*Frank Ney lights a flare during the bathtub festivities. Known as "Black Frank", the mayor of Nanaimo was the city's biggest champion and used the "stunt" of the race to put Nanaimo on the map.*

# Frank Ney's Nanaimo

Beside Swy-A-Lana Lagoon is a life-sized bronze statue of Frank Ney, the late mayor of Nanaimo, who was first elected in 1967. Rather than a dignified gentleman proudly arrayed in his robes of office, you'll discover a pirate captain holding his cutlass aloft as though preparing to board the enemy ship. It is a pose that captures the essence of this colourful and flamboyant man who brought Nanaimo to the attention of people right across the continent.

Frank Ney was a salesman, and the product he peddled was his community. Love him or not, he did everything he could to benefit Nanaimo, whether it was more parkland or an improved ferry service and vibrant economy.

Ney was born in England, on May 12, 1918. Raised in Winnipeg, Ney discovered hockey, and at 18 he returned to England to play and coach. When the Second World War broke out he ended up in the Royal Air Force and transferred to the RCAF near the end of the fighting. After the war Frank travelled to Nanaimo to join his uncle's real estate business. When his uncle moved to Victoria, Ney, along with his father, Frank Sr., as president and his brother, Bill, as partner, created the Great Nanaimo Land Trust, which quickly became one of Nanaimo's major developers.

His simple business card that read "Frank J. Ney, Real Estate Salesman" belied his energy and ambition in becoming the fourth-largest land developer in British Columbia. His firm developed 2,000 homesites in the Nanaimo area and two resorts on Gabriola Island in the 1950s.

Frank Ney is known as the man who brought a new vision to Nanaimo, expanding the city north along the Island Highway.

*Frank Ney fires the pistol to mark the beginning of the annual bathtub race.*

But for all his business acumen, Frank Ney will always be best known as "Black Frank," the man who made Nanaimo the "Bathtub Capital of the World." The inaugural World Championship Bathtub Race took place in 1967 to mark Canada's 100th birthday. Ney, who was centennial chairman, decided that Nanaimo needed to bring the city and Vancouver Island to the attention of the rest of Canada. It is doubtful that anyone could have foreseen how wildly the stunt would succeed. The next year the Bathtub Society gave Ney the honorary title of Admiral of the Fleet. For Ney the race was a year-round event. He donned his pirate's costume anywhere and any time he thought it might bring attention to Nanaimo and the bathtub race.

The popularity of the event reached its heyday in 1982, when Black Frank and his big bathtub went to Toronto for the annual Grey Cup parade. Ney showed up in his pirate outfit and talked to anyone who would listen about the glories of Nanaimo. It wasn't long before viewers across the country were tuning their televisions in on bathtub-weekend to watch the Nanaimo-to-Vancouver race.

Frank Ney was colourful and brash. He craved public attention, and approval. He was everywhere at once, and he wouldn't miss a birthday party, anniversary, or a council meeting. He loved to play with his 11 children and their friends. Even his political rivals couldn't help but respect a man who gave so much to his city.

The motto he created was: "Nanaimo, jewel of the west, sun porch of Canada, bathtub capital of the world." Ney believed every word and lived it every day.

He was bigger than life, yet treated everyone the same. When Queen Elizabeth and Prince Philip visited the mayor in his office, he plunked his pirate's hat on top of Prince Philip's head. Even the Queen gave a little smile.

Frank Ney also served as the Social Credit MLA from 1969 to 1972, was named Freeman of the City in 1984, and was re-elected as mayor in 1986. Just months before his death in 1992, after being diagnosed with an inoperable brain tumour, he showed up at the harbour on bathtub weekend in full pirate regalia. There is no doubt he would be pleased by the bronze statue at Swy-A-Lana Lagoon.

*Frank Ney, pirate's sword held aloft, stands guard over Swy-A-Lana Lagoon.*

*Parades throughout the year bring people downtown
to enjoy a weekend of family fun.*

*Spectators of all ages, buskers of all shapes and sizes, and the sound of music make for festive summer days in downtown Nanaimo.*

## Other Seasonal Festivals

In 2001 the Vancouver Island Symphony gave its first free concert in the park in the Lions Pavilion in Maffeo Sutton Park on the waterfront. The concert attracted 5,000 people, who enjoyed a wide variety of light classical music ending with Tchaikovsky's "1812 Overture". A highlight of this rousing piece of music was the finale, when the Royal Canadian Sea Cadets from HMCS *Quadra* summer camp in Comox fired their antique field guns. The **Symphony in the Harbour** is now an annual event that takes place early in August.

In late August, Nanaimo hosts the **Vancouver Island Exhibition**, a down-home country fair with everything from draft horses to giant pumpkins and enough exciting rides to keep kids and adults reeling for hours, takes place at the Beban Park fair grounds.

Early September brings the annual **Cans Food Festival** to Nanaimo's Old City Quarter. For the price of a donation to the food bank, visitors can taste delicious and exotic foods from a variety of excellent downtown restaurants while being entertained by local singers and dance troupes.

In mid-September, downtown Nanaimo goes for a walk on the wild side when local organizers stage the **Adventure Games**. The games include extreme sports like street luge and box jumping by BMX bikers. More traditional sports include an urban 5K run, a downhill mountain-bike event, a rock-climbing competition, and kayak races. Kids also participate in events like the soapbox derby and tricycle races. The event that probably draws the largest crowd of spectators is the wife-carrying contest. During the 300-yard course each man, carrying his wife upside down on his back, negotiates a water challenge and a deep-sand traverse, climbs over log obstacles, and then sprints as best he can to the finish line. A "fear factor" event is also part of the Adventure Games, with contestants undergoing challenges that focus on their worst fears.

*Maestro Marlin Wolfe conducts the Vancouver Island Symphony Orchestra in crowd-pleasing classics at the annual free Symphony in the Harbour concert at Swy-A-Lana Lagoon.*

The **Infringing Dance Festival** takes place while the Adventure Games are in full swing. Modern-dance performances are held in several downtown venues as well as on the streets. A highlight each year is the vertical dance troupe that performs on the rear wall of the Port Theatre facing Harbourfront Plaza.

In October Nanaimo hosts the **inFEST Film Festival,** a celebration of locally made shorts as well as longer films and documentaries from across the province.

Local oenophiles anticipate the annual **Wine Festival,** which takes place at Beban Park in late October and features tasting booths where you can sample the wares of dozens of wineries, including Vancouver Island's nationally recognized vineyards such as Chateau Wolff, Blue Grouse, Cherry Point, Divino, Alderlea, and Vigneti Zanatta.

Halloween in Nanaimo would not be Halloween without witches and ghosts decorating local homes and without hundreds of carved pumpkins lining the spooky shadows of the **Shady Mile** on Jingle Pot Road.

Christmas is marked by the glorious **Festival of Trees** in Beban Park. For four days in late November, dozens of gorgeously decorated trees stand on display in the Beban Park recreation centre. Events such as a "glitz and glamour" casino night, an afternoon tea, and a luncheon help raise funds for the Malaspina University-College Foundation.

The year of festivals and special events ends on December 31 with a giant **New Year's Eve** party sponsored by the New VI Television and the City of Nanaimo. Thousands of people throng Harbourfront Plaza to sip cocoa, dance to the music of local bands, and welcome in the New Year.

The Nanaimo Motocross Association is home to the Wastelands Motocross Park, a world-class racing facility located at the end of Weigles Road. In June the club hosts a leg of the **Pro-National Motocross Championship Series,** which draws riders and as many as 10,000 spectators from all over Canada and the United States.

*A BMX rider catches some big air at Nanaimo's Adventure Games. Daring BMX stunts are one of many exciting attractions at this annual downtown event.*

During one weekend each September, the downtown is closed to traffic as The Adventure Games take over the city streets. Events include daredevil skateboarding, BMX stunts, an urban run, a "fear factor" event, and even a wife-carrying contest. A beer garden and live music and dance add to the festivities.

# Parks and Recreation

## Parks

Nanaimo's parks are some of its greatest assets. With more than 1,100 hectares of parkland and protected open space, the City of Nanaimo offers residents and visitors many opportunities to enjoy the magnificence of nature.

**Beban Park** is Nanaimo's premier recreation centre, offering activities such as swimming, skating, tennis, basketball, golf, and lawn bowling, as well as playgrounds, multi-use trails, and playing fields. Its social centre provides space for community-group activities, meetings and seminars, and arts and crafts, including a pottery room and kiln. The 25-metre indoor pool offers classes for children, adults, and seniors, and there is a leisure pool with a tropical theme and a 61-metre water slide. Beban Park also features an indoor and outdoor equestrian area, a skating arena, and a BMX track that draws young bikers from all parts of the island. The park also has an 18-hole pitch-and-putt and a fenced off-leash dog area where dogs and their owners can socialize and play.

*Nanaimo is surrounded by unspoiled nature. The many parks in and around the city offer ample opportunity for birdwatching, strolling, or more strenuous hiking.*

*Rock climbing is a popular sport in Nanaimo. When enthusiasts aren't scaling the cliffs above the sea (left) or the Nanaimo River, they head to The Romper Room, Nanaimo's indoor climbing facility.*

**Bowen Park** is an enchanted forest located in the heart of the city. It features a scenic waterfall, meandering trails, a children's barnyard, an interpretive centre, a duck pond, an outdoor swimming pool, a disc golf course, a curling club, and the lush Hailey Rhododendron Grove, which boasts more than 350 species. Much of this forest in the city has been left undeveloped, and you are apt to encounter deer, beavers, otters, raccoons, pheasants, or grouse as you amble down the meandering trails past thick stands of cedar, hemlock, maple, and fir. The park also features a horseshoe pitch, lacrosse fields, tennis courts, a lawn-bowling green, and two covered picnic shelters. The recreation building offers rooms for arts and crafts and activities such as dancing and carpet bowling.

**Westwood Lake Park** at the foot of the Westwood Ridges and Mount Benson is Nanaimo's favourite swimming spot. This man-made lake has a sandy beach with shallow water for wading, as well as a raft for diving anchored out in deeper water. Circling the lake is one of the most popular walking trails in the city. The broad six-kilometre mulched trail runs south under tall cedars and firs and climbs up a rock bluff that affords excellent views of Mount Benson. It continues around the southern tip of the lake and along the west side, where a trail branches off to the Morrell Nature Sanctuary. Farther along, another path leads to the trail system that climbs the Westwood Ridges and goes to the top of Mount Benson. The main trail circles the north end of the lake, crosses a sturdy cedar bridge, and winds back along the east side of the lake to the beach. Fishers in canoes or in motorboats often ply the lake, casting their lines in hopes of snagging the cutthroat trout periodically stocked here.

**Colliery Dam Park** is situated just south of Malaspina University-College and is a popular swimming spot in summer and a serene retreat year-round—often the only sounds you will hear are waterfalls, songbirds, crickets, and frogs. Both the Parkway Trailway, a footpath that roughly parallels the Nanaimo Parkway, and the Trans Canada Trail cross this park. Gentle hiking trails wind through the cool woods that surround both the upper and lower lakes. Rugged rock outcroppings make perfect diving and sunning spots and often, if you're very still, you will see muskrats swimming in the waters along the shore.

*Bowen Park is a must-see for all newcomers to the city. Volume in the Millstone River waterfall varies with the seasons, but the river walk is popular year-round.*

*Colliery Dam Park is a quiet oasis in the city that offers trails through tall trees and sunny meadows beside still waters. The dam is stocked with cutthroat trout and gives novice fishers a good opportunity to try their hand at angling.*

**Diver Lake Park,** off Labieux Road in central Nanaimo, offers excellent walking trails, a playground, a fitness circuit, picnic tables, and a fishing dock.

**Swy-A-Lana Lagoon** is a saltwater lagoon in the heart of downtown that uses the natural ebb and flow of the tides to create a habitat for marine life. An arched pedestrian bridge leads from the lagoon to **Maffeo Sutton Park,** which has basketball courts, giant chessboards, a bandshell, sandlot playground, fishing pier, picnic tables, and several open grassy spaces for picnicking and playing. The views of the harbour are breathtaking. Maffeo Sutton Park is the site of many summertime activities, such as the Silly Boat Regatta and the Dragon Boat Festival.

**Buttertubs Marsh** is an 18-hectare bird and wildlife sanctuary located adjacent to the Millstone River near Bowen Park. A 4.5-kilometre walking trail circles the marsh, allowing you to enjoy the variety of plant and animal life that adds to the park's beauty. This is a favourite area of birdwatchers, particularly in the spring and fall when migratory flocks pass through. The marsh abounds in cedar waxwings, northern flickers, Virginia rails, mallards, spotted towhees, and belted kingfishers.

**Neck Point** is a 14.5-hectare waterfront park situated along Hammond Bay Road that is well known for its excellent trail system and amenities such as dive facilities, picnicking areas, and special lookouts that highlight the spectacular scenery surrounding the park. Neck Point was only selectively logged over the years before becoming a park, so old-growth trees abound, and many decaying trees serve as habitat for bats, squirrels, and raccoons. These trees are also important perches

*Neck Point has great settings for a quiet read, family beach trips, birding, and hiking.*

for bald eagles. If you know where to look, you can see several bald-eagle nests at Neck Point. Other trees are home to pileated woodpeckers, barn owls, and red squirrels, while a riparian area with decaying wood debris is home to the clouded salamander and various insects. For most visitors to Neck Point Park, the highlights of the trail system are the lookout points high on the cliffs. From here you can observe the waves crashing against the rocks below and take in the spectacular views of the snow-capped mountains of the mainland.

*Youngsters on field trips, as seen here in Bowen Park, are a common sight around Nanaimo.*

*Beachcombing is a favourite activity in Nanaimo. Starfish are often visible at low tide, like these two that turned up on Departure Bay beach.*

*Piper's Lagoon boasts a rare ecosystem of Garry oak meadows laced with trails that invite exploration.*

*Combined with the outer shoreline, this is a favourite beachcombing, walking, and windsurfing spot.*

Piper's Lagoon Park off Hammond Bay Road is built on an isthmus that extends out to a rocky headland. This eight-hectare park features twisting trails through a rare Garry oak ecosystem, which lead to a number of seaside lookouts ideal for watching seagulls, sandpipers, horned grebes, loons, kingfishers, oystercatchers, and great blue herons. A cove between two high rock outcroppings is sheltered from the winds and is a marvellous picnic spot. The broad path that leads to this prominent rocky headland is bordered by tall seagrasses and stunted trees bent landward by the force of the prevailing winds. These winds make Piper's Lagoon the most popular windsurfing area in the city. From the sandy beach, a favourite for swimming and beachcombing, you can observe surfers on their boards with colourful sails scudding across the waves.

Jack Point/Biggs Park is situated near the Duke Point ferry terminal. Although this park is the most remote from the centre of the city and is situated surprisingly close to an industrial park, it is well worth the trip. An underpass from the parking area leads to a broad path that hugs the shore and affords panoramic views of the Nanaimo River Estuary and the city, with Mount Benson forming a majestic backdrop. Soon the trail rises up the cliffs via a series of cedar steps and boardwalks, and you enter an old forest of cedars and firs. The

shoreline is broken by numerous small coves where sea ducks paddle. The trail winds past a remarkable, ancient arbutus tree whose trunk leans against a tall cedar, their leaves and branches intertwining in the canopy overhead. The trail continues through a grove of soaring cedars, the forest floor carpeted with ivy, and eventually ends at Jack Point, where the view opens up. Here you can see the Gabriola Island ferry travelling back and forth across the harbour, and on a clear day you can see for miles up Northumberland Channel.

Newcastle Island is a just short ferry ride across the harbour from downtown Nanaimo. The island is criss-crossed by nature trails that wind under tall stands of arbutus, Garry oak, and Douglas fir. A hiking trail that circles the island takes in the wild and rocky coastline, which is interspersed with sheltered coves. At low tide it is actually possible to wade across the channel between Protection and Newcastle islands. The old quarry and mine shafts echo the life of another era, while an old dance pavilion, erected in the 1940s, carries you back to the age of *The Great Gatsby*. Perhaps the most charming feature of the island is the sweeping lawn in front of the pavilion—a favourite with picnickers who come from Nanaimo by rowboat, powerboat, sailboat, or on the two ferries that ply the harbour during the warm summer months.

*The waters around Newcastle Island form a protected marine park and a favourite anchoring place for boats from up and down the west coast.*

# Newcastle Island

Newcastle Island is a park with great historic significance. Once the site of an operating mine and a quarry where millstones were manufactured, it was also recognized as a haven of unspoiled wilderness, beaches, and trails. For years it was a favourite with local picnickers, who rowed out across the harbour, and from 1913 to 1920 it was the site of the annual Miners' Picnic. The CPR purchased it in 1931 and promoted it in the hope of luring tourists north from Victoria.

By 1937 the CPR declared that "in a brief four years Newcastle Island has become British Columbia's favourite outing spot." The promotional literature called Newcastle Island an idyllic jewel on the "Gulf Coast Riviera."

Gas rationing virtually put an end to tourist activity during the war years, and when the federal government requisitioned the CPR's ships, *Princess Kathleen* and *Princess Marguerite*, which had ferried passengers back and forth, Newcastle Island became difficult to access.

After the war, Newcastle Island did not regain its former popularity. It was the age of the automobile, and a family vacation meant never having to abandon your vehicle. For years, Newcastle Island was simply a beautiful and remote spot in the harbour. Then Nanaimo acquired the island from the CPR in 1955, and in 1961 the city granted it to the provincial government, which turned it into a marine park.

*Newcastle Island, a provincial park, is a favourite local escape. The island, easily accessed by a ferry leaving from Nanaimo's harbour, has camping facilities, picnic grounds, beaches, miles of hiking trails, and a historic dance pavilion.*

**Cable Bay Trail** is one of Nanaimo's newer parks and is located near Cedar-by-the-Sea, a small community south of Nanaimo. A 30-minute walk takes you on a trail that winds gently down from the parking lot through a forest of alder, western red hemlock, maple, cedar, and fir to Cable Bay.

During the winter months, the sound of barking sea lions tells you that you are approaching the bay. Harmac's log booms are stored in the water near the bay and are a favourite wintering ground for the large aquatic mammals. Harbour seals are also plentiful in these waters. A narrow trail continues past the Cable Bay trail and hugs the shore heading south to Dodd Narrows. This is a magnificent vantage point for observing marine life.

**Hemer Park** is located in the village of Cedar and offers many kilometres of easy walking trails past Holden Lake, where fishermen angle for cutthroat trout, and through an old forest where many of the towering cedars and Douglas firs are hundreds of years old. A beaver pond is a favourite of migrating waterfowl, including white trumpeter swans. An observation platform makes birdwatching particularly rewarding here.

**Linley Valley** lies in the last large area of undeveloped land in the city. Through the tireless efforts of the Nanaimo Area Land Trust, supported by the City of Nanaimo, Linley Valley became Nanaimo's newest major park in 2003. Linley Valley is home to an abundance of wildlife, including deer, beaver, frogs, bald eagles, hawks, and some of the rarest songbirds in the area. Several kilometres of walking trails allow excellent access through the park. The main trail from the end of Linley Road follows Cottle Creek to Cottle Lake, a small, tranquil lake inhabited by cutthroat trout, beaver, and waterfowl. Other trails include the Fir Traverse, the Cedar Crosscut, and the Arbutus Bluffs, which begins with a very steep climb at its western end and offers a view at the eastern end that makes the climb well worthwhile.

In addition to these major parks, the City of Nanaimo, through its volunteers in the parks program that supports citizens in creating neighbourhood parks, boasts dozens of smaller parks scattered throughout the city. In many neighbourhoods, these parks fill the function of village greens. They contain playgrounds, benches, and often, playing fields.

*Hemer Provincial Park, minutes south of Nanaimo, features extensive, shaded hiking trails, a beaver pond, and a pretty lake stocked with cutthroat trout.*

## Nanaimo Aquatic Centre

Nanaimo's Aquatic Centre is far more than just a pool. Opened in June 2001, the centre boasts the largest wave pool west of West Edmonton Mall, a steam room, sauna room, three waterslides, a lazy river, an interactive fishing boat, a multi-purpose room, a fitness room, café, and more. One Aquatic Centre water-slide is the highest indoor slide in British Columbia. There is enough concrete in the facility to build a 15-storey apartment building.

Its lofty ceilings, bright windows, and excellent lighting make going to the Nanaimo Aquatic Centre feel like a trip to the beach. The interactive fishing boat is the biggest pool toy most children have ever played with. There are valves to turn, water to squirt, hoses to play with, and rungs to climb on, over, and through. A seal, an orca, and a fish spout water into the pool, while colourful banners add to the festive spirit of the centre.

The leisure aspect of the centre is pure fun, but there's another side to Nanaimo's premier aquatic facility—a 52-metre Olympic lap pool that is flexible enough to set up as two 25-metre tanks with shallow ends that can be raised and lowered from 0 to 2.5 metres. There is also a dive tank with a one- and a three-metre diving board.

After an hour or a day of swimming laps or zipping down the slides, weary water babies can relax in the 40-person hot tub or at the poolside café.

## Trails for Hiking and Biking

Nanaimo's goal is to give residents and visitors the best possible access to a wide range of outdoor activities and to nature itself. Whether you want an easy bike ride, a walk along a smooth paved path, or a steep climb through rugged wilderness, you'll find it in and around the Harbour City.

The **Parkway Trailway** is the backbone of Nanaimo's paved trail system and links Aulds Road in the north to Chase River 20 kilometres to the south, roughly following the entire length of the Nanaimo Parkway. This tree-lined corridor provides safe and convenient access to many points of interest in the city. Signs point to popular destinations like Buttertubs Marsh, Colliery Dam, Bowen Park, and the harbour via

the **Millstone Trail**. The Parkway Trailway also connects to Malaspina University-College, the Aquatic Centre, and major shopping centres.

The **E & N Trail** is one of Nanaimo's newest paved trails and is still growing. This convenient path parallels the E & N railway track, which runs alongside the Island Highway (the main artery running through the city). The trail gives pedestrians and cyclists safe access to Beban Park and several major shopping centres.

If you prefer more rugged hiking, go to **Westwood Lake Park** and walk around to the west side of the lake, where signs point you toward the Westwood Ridges. A large network of trails runs through the valley floor between the ridges that overlook Westwood Lake and the lower slopes of Mount Benson. The valley trails are a favourite of cyclists. Hikers prefer to head for the high ridges with their spectacular views of the city from the rocky bluffs. The first ridge provides an excellent viewpoint and picnic site. A further 45-minute hike down and then up the steep second ridge provides views of Ladysmith to the south. The trail continues down to the **Morrell Nature Sanctuary**, where the trail system joins once again with the path that curls around Westwood Lake.

More ambitious hikers may want to tackle **Mount Benson**, which looms like a giant guarding Nanaimo's western borders. The most popular access point for the peak is from the back of Westwood Lake. This steep trail follows old logging roads in part and is generally well flagged. **Cougar Bluff** with its fixed rope climb is a dramatic but safe feature

*The Aquatic Centre, with over 2.7 million litres of water in its pools, is one of Nanaimo's favourite "watering holes." Along with an Olympic-sized lap pool, it offers three indoor water slides, a wave pool, and water toys for children of all ages. The 32 overhead banners represent the work of nine local artists.*

of this trail. Another popular access route to the peak starts at the end of Benson View Road, where the trail circles the end of pretty **Mystic Lake** and branches to the right for a steep two-hour pitch to the top. In the spring, snow runoff forms a roaring river down the rocky slopes near the trail. This is also the trailhead for one of Nanaimo's most popular mountain-bike parks, which boasts myriad obstacles and steep slopes to challenge even the most expert rider.

**The Abyss**, off Harewood Mines Road in Nanaimo's south end, is another favourite of mountain bikers. The trail is so named because it runs beside a narrow cleft created by an earthquake that occurred many years ago and left a 300-foot-deep fissure in the rock. Hikers have also discovered the pleasure of The Abyss, and it now forms part of the **Trans Canada Trail**.

For a short hike to Nanaimo's most spectacular destination, drive to the end of Doumont Road in the city's north end. Park your car and take a short 20-minute hike through a pristine forest to **Ammonite Falls** in the Benson Creek Regional Park. The 85-foot falls tumble off the ridges of Mount Benson into a clear pool lined with rocks and shaded by tall trees. The falls are named after the ammonite fossils found in this area, many of them dating back more than 70 million years.

*A short hike through a lush forest leads to beautiful Ammonite Falls, named after the ancient fossils that have been found in the Nanaimo area.*

*The Nanaimo area abounds with trails for mountain bikers, including the famous "Abyss," named after a cleft created by an earthquake that occurred many years ago.*

*Scuba diving is a popular sport in Nanaimo. The area's waters attract divers from all over the world. The Nanaimo Dive Association has helped create the world's largest artificial reef by sinking several old Navy ships. The wrecks are easily accessed and offer a fascinating underwater world to explore.*

## Diving

Nanaimo attracts divers from around the world. One Nanaimo dive operator calls the city "the best dive destination in the known universe." Dodd Narrows and Gabriola Passage share the honour of being named the number-two dive places in B.C. for marine life and biodiversity by the readers of *Rodale's Scuba Diving*, a highly respected American publication.

In the waters just outside Nanaimo's harbour, the Nanaimo Dive Association (NDA) has created what local divers call "the Whistler of diving." In the mid-1990s the NDA acquired a naval ship, the former HMCS *Saskatchewan*, and began a massive cleanup of the vessel in preparation for sinking it. Hundreds of volunteers removed paint, scrap metal, wiring, lighting fixtures, old equipment, furniture, and everything else that was not

nailed or screwed down, and on June 14, 1997, the NDA, with the help of the Cousteau Society, sank the *Saskatchewan*.

The former HMCS *Cape Breton*, after a similar cleanup operation, was sunk on October 20, 2001, creating the world's largest artificial reef. The reef rapidly became inhabited by sea life, making it a destination for thousands of divers each year, many of them coming during the winter months when visibility is at its peak.

Next on the NDA's agenda is the sinking of the *Rivtow Lion*, a retired 147-foot naval tug that will be sunk in the shallow waters of Departure Bay to become a training ground for divers who want to explore the *Saskatchewan* and *Cape Breton*.

The only local dive locations that can rival Nanaimo's artificial reef are its natural sites. Dodd Narrows is situated five nautical miles southeast of Nanaimo. The fast currents in this narrow channel create an ideal habitat for a lush assortment of colourful marine invertebrates, including many species of sea anemone, aggregating anemone, sea stars, mosshead warbonnets, Puget Sound king crab, orange cup corals, red Irish lords, and rock cod. During the winter months, divers can watch Steller's sea lions feasting on salmon in the swift tidal stream.

Snake Island, just outside Nanaimo's harbour, is a bird sanctuary with a wall dive starting in 20 metres of water and descending to over 200 metres. Divers can observe colonies of cloud sponges and plumose anemones or interact with a large colony of friendly harbour seals that has made this area its home.

At Jesse Island, located in Departure Bay, divers can take advantage of three distinct sites in sheltered conditions. Each site features a unique ecology ranging from rock pillars and sea caves to bottom slopes and pinnacles. Marine life varies in each location and includes sea pens, sea whips, plumose anemones, rare crimson anemones, sea perch, capazone, wolf eels, and octopuses.

Neck Point off Hammond Bay Road in Nanaimo provides divers with a land-based site. A narrow neck of rock and sand juts out into the Strait of Georgia, allowing divers to enter quickly into deep water. A paved road leads through Neck Point Park to the dive site, making accessibility easy even for people in wheelchairs.

Four Fathom Reef, known as a spawning ground for all species of rockfish, lingcod, capazone, spiny pink scallops, and giant Pacific octopuses, and Clarke Rock with its dual pinnacles that rise as high as three metres beneath the surface, are two other popular Nanaimo dive sites. All of these locations offer crystal-clear water, excellent visibility, and an abundance of plant and animal life, including the occasional docile six-gill shark.

*Sea lions make the rocks, islands, and log booms in Nanaimo's harbour their winter home.*

# Local Treasures

Nanaimo and its surrounding villages and rural areas are full of surprises and hidden delights. If you own a sturdy pair of hiking shoes, you can tramp on trails for days. Some will provide you with a short, invigorating walk, while others, like the steep route to the top of Mount Benson, will give you an excellent workout. But you don't have to plunge into the wilderness to discover local attractions that often only the residents know about.

## Nanaimo Fish Hatchery

Just south of town near the Cassidy Inn is the Nanaimo Fish Hatchery, with walking trails along Napoleon Creek and through the surrounding woods. Starting in October, visitors can watch salmon in their natural habitat. Thousands of chum salmon spawn each year below the hatchery fish ladder. Visitors may also tour the hatchery's interpretive centre and learn about the different species of salmon that live in the waters around Nanaimo.

Since its inception in 1979, the Nanaimo Fish Hatchery has produced more than 20 million fry and smolts, including chinook, coho, chum, and pink salmon, as well as steelhead and cutthroat trout.

*The Barton & Leier Gallery in Yellow Point is a favourite destination for lovers of art and artistic gardens. Artists Grant Leier and his wife Nixie Barton have achieved national recognition.*

*The friendly animals are just one of the attractions of the Shady Mile Farm Market on Jingle Pot Road.*

## The Bungy Zone

The Bungy Zone, about 10 minutes south of Nanaimo, has the distinction of being North America's first legal bungy bridge. Saunders Bridge, 143 feet above the Nanaimo River, was custom-built especially for bungy jumping. Thrill seekers make the pilgrimage to the Bungy Zone from all over the world, many to take part in the Zone's annual nude jump for charity.

Although the Bungy Zone now boasts three adrenaline-pumping events, the original bungy jump, with a headfirst dive 143 feet straight down, still looms as the most formidable. The Ultimate Swing pulls you across the canyon at speeds of up to 140 kilometres per hour, and The Flying Fox extends in a 600-foot-deep arc along the canyon, with participants reaching speeds of up to 100 kilometres per hour.

For those who are not yet ready to make the big jump, the Bungy Zone provides viewing and picnicking areas on its scenic grounds.

## The Shady Mile

The Shady Mile refers to a stretch of Jingle Pot Road that winds through rolling farm fields at the foot of Mount Benson. This green, leafy mile is transformed each year on Halloween as shadowy figures flit under the trees to place lighted jack-o'-lanterns on stumps and old fence posts. In the darkness, hundreds of grinning and ghoulish faces delight those who make the annual pilgrimage to see them.

During the rest of the year, people drive down the Shady Mile with a different destination in mind. One of Nanaimo's hidden treasures is the **Shady Mile Market**, a rustic farm market selling fresh produce, fruits, and berries. On the surrounding seven-acre property is a 10,000-square-foot greenhouse complex where the owners grow several varieties of vegetables including tomatoes, cucumbers, and peppers.

The market also features giftware made by local artisans and a coffee and ice-cream bar with outdoor seating. But the

*The Bungy Zone, long considered one of North America's premier bungy jumping sites, provides three distinct thrills for those who dare.*

market's biggest draw is the farm, where children can pet and feed chickens, goats, sheep, alpacas, ducks, rabbits, ponies, and other creatures that have been rescued from unsuitable homes. There is always a mother hen with her brood of chicks underfoot somewhere in the market, and one hen that insists on laying her daily egg in a bin inside the store.

## Nanaimo's Own Vineyard

Chateau Wolff is off the beaten wine path on Vancouver Island. Located just outside Nanaimo, it is the island's most northern vineyard and the only producing winery in the community.

When Harry von Wolff bought the land for his vineyard in 1987, he had already been dreaming about it for 30 years. He believed there was a need for a high-quality, locally made wine—wine that would be made from naturally grown grapes, without using chemicals or additives of any kind.

He began nurturing a few grapevines from France and Germany in the early '70s, and in 1987 he found the perfect eight acres of land near the end of Maki Road, which runs off East Wellington Road near the western city limits.

Two years later, von Wolff began to sell his wine, and he now runs a thriving little farm-gate winery, selling Pinot Noir, Grand Rouge Demi-Sec, Pinot Blanc, Viva, and Grand Rouge liqueur wine to neighbours, tourists, friends, and, on occasion, restaurateurs. He produces seven tons of grapes each year, which translates into about 6,000 bottles of wine.

## Yellow Point

South of town just past the village of Cedar, Yellow Point Road and Cedar Road form a circle drive that takes you through one of Vancouver Island's prettiest rural communities. Here tall stands of trees are interspersed with rolling farmland, small seaside resorts, and funky cottages. At many farm gateways are rough wooden stands displaying free-range eggs, cut flowers, bunches of fresh herbs, giant squash, and sometimes homemade crafts.

During the summer months, locals sell fresh produce, home-baked bread, buns and cookies, and crafts at the **Cedar Farmers' Market** near the entrance to the **Crow and Gate Pub** on Yellow Point Road.

The farmers' market and the pub aren't the only stops of interest on the Yellow Point tour. Colourful signs lead to galleries, artisans' homes, and pretty gift shops. The **Barton & Leier Gallery** is a favourite, with its funky baroque garden filled with trees, shrubs, and flowers as well as statues, fountains, garden structures, sculptures, and other pieces of art. The gallery is home to the art of Grant Leier and Nixie Barton, whose work has become well known across Canada. Grant Leier's paintings are distinguished by a vivid use of colour, while Nixie Barton's style is full of rich texture and luminous tones.

**Hazelwood Herb Farm** is another favourite stop along the Yellow Point circuit. Hundreds of varieties of herbs grow in great profusion in the formal demonstration garden as well as under a slatted roof and in the test beds. A pond and gazebo invite visitors to linger and breathe the mingled scents of basil, thyme, peppermint, and lavender. The shop offers an extensive array of soaps, bubble baths, vinegars, oils, sachets, and luscious gift baskets.

In late summer, the **Trudell Blueberry Farm** opens its fields to allow visitors to pick what might arguably be the fattest, juiciest, and sweetest blueberries in the province, and in early fall the nearby **McNab Farm** invites children and adults to lose themselves in its giant corn maze.

**Roberts Memorial Park** is a small treasure on this route. A trail of less than a kilometre under towering cedars and Douglas firs leads from the parking lot at Yellow Point Road to the beach, where the waves have smoothed the rocks, carved shallow hollows, and washed up massive logs. In the spring, sky-blue scilla carpets the ground. **Yellow Point Park** offers another pretty stroll through a forest and is a favourite with local equestrians.

Foresters everywhere regard **Wildwood** as the world icon of sustainable forestry. Now owned by The Land Conservancy of British Columbia, Wildwood is still the home of Merve Wilkinson, who has practised his unique brand of forestry here for more than 60 years. Saturday-afternoon tours lead visitors under the massive trees, many of them almost 1,000 years old, and past the stands of newly sprouting cedars and Douglas firs.

Not far from Wildwood is historic **Yellow Point Lodge**, situated on the jutting cape of land that gives the area its name. The lodge is a tall post-and-beam structure anchored to the rock. Jerry Hill, father of the current owner, Richard, built the lodge in 1939. At that time, the 165-acre property was surrounded by wilderness. As well as the rustic lodge, Jerry Hill built cabins on the beach and in the woods. In 1985 the log building burned down, and the Hill family replaced it with the current structure, which has a soaring roof held up by massive beams. The common room is dominated by a giant rock fireplace and by the view of the ocean, inches away from the windows that surround the room.

If you stray from the main Yellow Point and Cedar roads, you may come across a dock on the shore of **Quennell Lake** where you can rent a canoe or kayak to explore the hidden coves on this long, many-fingered body of water. Or you may stop at **Yellow Point Country Gardens,** where you can wrap up armfuls of bright dried flowers; or you may discover a farm that breeds Canadian horses, or perhaps just a dirt road that ends at a stand of trees or a meadow perfect for a leisurely picnic and an afternoon nap. Yellow Point is that sort of place.

## Protection Island

The Protection Island ferry leaves every hour from the downtown harbour to take passengers to the floating **Dinghy Dock Pub** or to the charming, eccentric, and often quixotic homes on this small island in Nanaimo's harbour. There is no car ferry to the island; the preferred method of transportation for residents is the electric golf cart. Two waterfront parks on the island are favourite stopovers for kayakers and for picnickers on a sunny afternoon. Still, the main attraction during the summer months is the floating pub with its extraordinary views of the city, its spectacular sunsets, its lively local entertainment, and its great pub food.

*Due to Nanaimo's mild climate, golfers enjoy playing year round on many excellent golf courses stretching from Cottonwood in Cedar to Fairwinds in Nanoose.*

*The Protection Connection ferry plies its way back and forth between Nanaimo's Harbour and Protection Island, where the floating Dinghy Dock Pub is the main attraction. Protection Island is also home to many artists, writers, and musicians.*

*The Yellow Point Lodge perches on a point of land surrounded by the sea.
This serene and rustic getaway has attracted vacationers for generations.*

*Hazelwood Herb Farms display gardens show off
hundreds of varieties of culinary and medicinal plants.*

# The Crow and Gate Pub

The Crow and Gate is a popular destination for visitors to Vancouver Island. The pub was built in 1972 by Jack Nash, who came to Canada from Sussex, England. It was the first licensed neighbourhood pub in British Columbia and a radical departure from the regular beer parlours everyone was used to. Nash was determined to replicate some of the best country pubs in England: no big-screen television sets for him. He wanted a pub where people would gather in the evening or at lunchtime, pick up a good mug of beer and some hearty pub food, and sit around an open fire at long tables or stroll out into the garden on a sunny day.

He was a meticulous craftsman and took great care in building the post-and-beam structure. Instead of using nails and screws, he pegged the floors and roof. He built long tables of massive slabs of cedar and benches to match. In the centre of the main room stands a fireplace that consumes great logs and is the preferred seating place in the winter months. When visitors drive up to the car park in front of the pub, they are likely to be greeted by Muscovy ducks or geese ambling to and from the pond. A long arbour hung with wisteria and Silver Lace vine leads to the brick entry and the imposing front door. The surrounding gardens are filled with roses, rhododendrons, azaleas, and pots of colourful annuals. Although Jack Nash is no longer the owner, he didn't just succeed in duplicating the atmosphere of a cozy English country pub, he surpassed it—and not a single customer has ever complained about the lack of television.

*The Crow and Gate pub in rural Yellow Point is Nanaimo's first neighbourhood pub. Its "old English" atmosphere make it a popular attraction.*

## Gabriola Island

The Gabriola Island ferry leaves the downtown Nanaimo dock for the 20-minute ride across the harbour roughly every hour. This is a popular day-trip destination for cyclists, picnickers, kayakers, and gallery hoppers.

The island is home to many talented painters, potters, silversmiths, weavers, poets, authors, quilters, and a host of other artisans. Many of them have small galleries and shops open to the public, and some even display their wares at small roadside tables. Payment for purchases is often on the honour system.

Gabriola is also home to marinas, pubs, a theatre, a jazz café, and the **Haven Resort**, which offers concerts, a spa, and seaside accommodation. Bed-and-breakfast homes and inns also abound here.

Silva Bay and Degnen Bay provide anchorage and mooring facilities for visiting boaters. **Gabriola Sands Provincial Park** provides a safe, sandy beach for swimming, and the **Gabriola Island Golf and Country Club** boasts a scenic nine-hole golf course.

Hikers can walk from one end of Gabriola to the other along a central spine of high ground while enjoying panoramic views and tranquil woodlands. Birdwatching is another popular activity on the island, given its population of bald eagles and migratory water birds. The calm waters to the southwest provide an excellent area for kayaking to the **Malaspina Galleries**, which is a must-see. This site, which features dramatic sandstone formations carved by the waves, is also accessible by foot.

But for many people, cycling is still the ideal form of transportation on Gabriola Island. Families and small groups can circumnavigate the island in several hours, perhaps longer if they pause to take in all the charming rural views of rolling farmland, tall trees, and hidden bays. It's also tempting to stray from the main road circling the island to explore country roads that end at old farm gates or perhaps at sheltered coves that offer a perfect invitation to do some beachcombing.

## Nanoose

A short drive north of Nanaimo is another pretty rural community called Nanoose. If you like hiking, make **Notch Hill** or **Enos Lake** your destination. The trailheads for both are on the main road heading toward the Fairwinds community and golf course.

Notch Hill is so named because a deep cleft divides the twin summits. The top of each involves a short but strenuous uphill climb through beautiful Garry oak meadows, where tall grasses rustle in the late-summer heat. The top of the east summit is slightly higher and affords excellent views south to Nanaimo and north to snow-capped Mount Arrowsmith. You are also likely to spot eagles on the treetops and possibly a shy deer in the underbrush. A rippling stream flows through the notch between the two peaks, and a bridge leads to the trail that ascends the western peak. Notch Hill boasts two distinct ecosystems: The eastern slopes support a rich undergrowth of ferns and wildflowers, while the exposed western slopes show bare rocks and tufted dried grass.

Enos Lake is a long finger of water bordered by forest. An intricate trail system circles the lake and branches off into the surrounding ponds and brush, making for varied and interesting walks and hikes. Enos Lake is also a favourite spot for paddlers.

Follow the road to **Fairwinds Golf and Country Club**. Fairwinds is the most temperate golf course in Canada and is open year-round. The course, designed by Les Furber, is situated against a backdrop of natural beauty where views of forests and the ocean are never far away. Wildlife also abounds

*The Gabriola Island Ferry makes frequent runs to Nanaimo's harbour. Gabriola offers charming beaches and parks and is also a mecca for cyclists.*

*Local kayakers like to set out from Nanaimo's harbour or from its beaches to explore the surrounding Gulf Islands. Rock formations like this one on DeCourcey Island are typical of the shoreline.*

*Gabriola Island is a favourite destination for kayakers. The island offers many beaches where weary paddlers can pull into shore and enjoy a lunch, a snooze, or a swim in tranquil waters.*

and you are likely to spot quail, deer, and eagles as you walk down the fairway.

A drive through the rural roads of Nanoose will eventually bring you to **Nanoose Edibles**, a certified organic farm that welcomes visitors year-round. The fields that border the road are laid out in orderly rows, and even on a grey January morning bright green leaves and shoots poke through the earth. Raspberry canes are neatly strung to their supports, and in the orchard, trees line up like soldiers waiting for inspection.

A rutted driveway leads to the market stand where, even in winter, fresh certified organic produce including leeks, kale, cabbage, collards, and the famous Nanoose Edibles mixed baby greens is available. During the summer months, the garden stand overflows with berries, greens, carrots, squash, beans, peas, and other colourful vegetables, as well as certified organic eggs from the farm's flock.

The Ebells, who own the 23-acre farm, welcome children to explore and taste raspberries fresh from the cane or carrots yanked from the earth and rinsed clean of soil. In early fall each year, a harvest festival takes place on the grounds of the farm, with local artists, musicians, wineries, and restaurants celebrating the bounty of the land.

*The Gabriola Island ferry's regular schedule of sailings makes this Gulf Island a convenient destination for day trips.*

*The City of Nanaimo has built many kilometres of paved trails and, to the delight of local cyclists, continues to add more to its network each year.*

## A Rich Sports Tradition

Nanaimo loves its teams and its team sports. People turn out to watch hockey at the Civic Arena or to cheer on the Mariners at the basketball court at Malaspina University-College, or to take in slo-pitch and baseball games at any one of a dozen or more diamonds scattered around the city.

The Clipper name is a proud one that goes back to the 1940s to a senior men's hockey team that won a national championship during that decade. The Nanaimo Clippers, Nanaimo's Junior A team since 1972, packs the Civic Arena with cheering fans throughout the season. The Clippers won the provincial championship in 1976, 1977, and 1978, and in 2004 the Clippers made it to the national championship tournament.

Nanaimo is also well known for its lacrosse teams. In the 1950s the senior teams were the Luckys and then the Labatts. Today the senior lacrosse team, the Nanaimo Timbermen, has a big following and consistently puts in a strong showing. The Timbermen won the provincials in 2003 and 2004.

The Mariners teams at Malaspina University-College provide significant provincial competition in men's and women's soccer, basketball, and volleyball. The women's volleyball team is dominant in British Columbia, having won six provincial championships in a row. Both the men's and women's Mariners soccer teams and basketball teams have won national championships within the last 15 years.

Swim teams are also strong in Nanaimo. The Riptides and White Rapids swim clubs have strong participation, while the Ebbtides is a masters team that attracts older swimmers who still want to swim competitively.

Youth soccer and minor baseball are strong. High school basketball and football teams put in a particularly impressive showing each year. Football didn't come to Vancouver Island until 1998. John Barsby Secondary School in Nanaimo was one of the first two high schools on Vancouver Island to introduce football to its sports program, and two years later the team won the provincial championship.

Nanaimo's rowing teams and canoe and kayak athletes are highly competitive. Leigh Dewar is a national champion and a Pan American games champion in canoe/kayak competitions.

In 2002 Nanaimo hosted the B.C. Summer Games, which officials declared among the best ever. Nanaimo also hosted the Royal Bank cup for Junior A hockey in 1998. As a host city, Nanaimo's professionalism is unparalleled.

*The Nanaimo Clippers, the city's Junior A hockey team, boasts a loyal following with big turnouts at all the home games.*

*Nanaimo has an excellent junior soccer program for boys and girls,*
*with active participation at all age levels.*

# Into the Future

Nanaimo's former resource-based economy is changing rapidly. The Harbour City that depended first on coal mining and later on the pulp industry now attracts tourists, artists, filmmakers, and high-tech innovators. The "new" Nanaimo economy is based on advanced technology, knowledge-based business, tourism, arts and culture, film and video production, and value-added manufacturing.

Nanaimo's skilled workforce and its superior training facilities at Malaspina University-College are two of its greatest assets. Nanaimo also boasts one of the most unusual coalitions of dedicated business people in the province. The Economic Development Group (EDG) is an organization of committed leaders within the community (including local government, business people, Malaspina University-College, The Nanaimo Port Authority, and Human Resources Canada), working together to ensure that Nanaimo is a community of social and economic opportunity. EDG provides leadership and a collective voice for economic development issues impacting Nanaimo. In 1999 EDG developed and adopted an Economic Development Strategy designed to guide Nanaimo successfully into the future.

*Nanaimo's busy harbour is home to commercial boats as well as thousands of pleasure craft.*

*Charming boutiques, restaurants, tea houses, and coffee shops line Nanaimo's waterfront walkway.*

# Malaspina University-College

From its beginning as a community college in 1969, Malaspina University-College has grown into an internationally recognized institution of higher learning, with four campuses and more than 9,800 full and part-time students registered in credit programs, and 10,500 enrolled in general interest courses.

Students at Malaspina University-College can earn a Bachelor's degree, a Master of Business Administration in partnership with the University of Hertfordshire in England, a Master of Education (rural studies) in conjunction with James Cook University in Northern Queensland, Australia, or take a wide variety of technical, career and trade programs leading to a diploma or certificate.

For sheer beauty, the Nanaimo campus (largest of the four), located on a spectacular 110-acre site on the lower slopes of Mount Benson, is second to none in the province. It features breathtaking views of Nanaimo Harbour, the Strait of Georgia and the coastal mountains on British Columbia's mainland.

Noteworthy features of the Nanaimo campus include two picturesque Japanese gardens donated by the Tamagawa University and Okayama Women's College in Japan, the Nanaimo Art Gallery on Campus, a performing arts theatre, library, fish hatchery, and museum of natural history. The internationally renowned Culinary Arts program at Malaspina University-College uses the cafeteria as a training opportunity for the students.

Because of its international reputation for its quality of programs and services, Malaspina University-College is host to more than 1,500 international students from over 40 countries around the globe. These students benefit from the friendly, personal approach to education that Malaspina provides. In turn, Canadian students benefit from the international contacts made by the University-College, giving them the opportunity to complete practica and field schools overseas.

Garden lovers will want to visit the 28-hectare Milner Gardens and Woodland located in nearby Qualicum Beach. The gardens were acquired by Malaspina University-College in 1996 from the late Victoria Milner, a descendent of the First Duke of Marlborough and thus related to the late Diana, Princess of Wales.

Malaspina's athletic teams consistently place in the top 10 in B.C. and Canada, while students and instructors of the Culinary Arts and Hairdressing certificate programs are regular recipients of gold medals in national and international competitions. Graduates of academic programs have been accepted into major Canadian and American graduate schools, where they have gone on to win scholarships and awards.

The strategy provides a set of economic goals for the city—a yardstick against which mayor and council as well as corporations and organizations can measure their decisions. EDG dubbed the strategy "The Circle of Prosperity" because it links economic prosperity with quality of life. The rationale behind the "circle" is that Nanaimo's physical beauty and lifestyle attract new residents; these people contribute to the economy, which in turn provides the city with more revenue to continue improving quality of life.

The economic goals identified by the EDG as essential for a prosperous future are:

**Committed leadership** A healthy community depends on leaders who care about the growth of the community and who understand that quality of life is tied to economic prosperity.

**Excellent foundations for growth** These include a business-friendly climate, one that supports existing businesses and welcomes new ones into the community. This welcoming atmosphere is created by the attitudes of residents, businesses, and local government. The EDG pays particular attention to small businesses, because these are the backbone of a community and frequently face greater challenges than do large corporations.

Businesses that drive the local economy and bring in new wealth from outside the community are also important focuses for the EDG. As Nanaimo expands its base of these economic drivers, residents and businesses will both benefit.

**Quality infrastructure** A solid city infrastructure relies on a skilled workforce as much as it does on physical structures. Technology is changing more rapidly than ever, and one of today's biggest challenges is keeping up with those changes. As in other communities, Nanaimo's workforce must constantly update its skills to keep up with industry demands. The most effective way to do that is for educational institutions to join with industry in fulfilling training needs.

*Many commercial fishing boats set out to sea from Nanaimo's harbour. Some sell their catch directly to the public at the Fisherman's Market, open daily in the harbour on Float "F".*

# Harmac

Harmac was the dream of Harry Reginald (H.R.) MacMillan, who was born in Ontario. In 1907, after graduating from the forestry program at Yale University, H.R. came to British Columbia to work as a timber cruiser. He fell in love with the west coast and its magnificent stands of fir, cedar, and hemlock trees. But he was incensed with the shoddy and wasteful practices of the forest industry. "Why bother conserving the forest?" was the prevailing philosophy. After all, there were endless stands of timber.

H.R. disagreed. He may have been the first man to call the forest a crop and the first to advance the idea that you have to replace what you take. His two main goals were to develop parks and protected places to ensure that the forest would not disappear, and to implement a code of forest practices.

In 1912 H.R. became chief forester of B.C., but after a few short years he quit in disgust; the red tape and bureaucracy were too much for him. H.R. wanted action, so he decided to build a lumber and pulp operation in which nothing was wasted. He found a location seven miles south of Nanaimo that had the three conditions he needed to create his model mill: a reliable supply of water from the Nanaimo River, a deep-water harbour on Northumberland Channel, and a trained labour force.

The town of Nanaimo was ecstatic that H.R. had chosen this site. The newspapers were full of glowing reports, and the out-of-work miners and their families were relieved. In 1948 he began construction on the mill, and in 1950 the first bale of unbleached pulp came off the rollers.

The conditions at Harmac in 1950 were primitive compared to today. Environmental standards were considered an expensive nuisance, and after the town's initial love affair with the mill wore off and the smell of the pulp-milling process reached the noses of Nanaimo-ites, the newspapers complained long and loud. But they never complained about the mill itself—nor did the people, regardless of the conditions under which they had to work and live. As far as they were concerned, Harmac had saved their town.

*The mill is still central to Nanaimo's economy, a significant part of its past and its future.*

*Freighters from around the world dock at Nanaimo's commercial boat basin. Duke Point south of Nanaimo provides barge-loading facilities and a container crane.*

Physical infrastructure is of course critically important as well, as it connects businesses to their markets locally and worldwide. Businesses that drive the economy sell to markets outside the local area, relying on effective communication and transportation links with the Lower Mainland, the United States, and the rest of the world.

Nanaimo's natural beauty and amenities are also strong components of the city's infrastructure, making it a desirable location in which to live and work. Businesses benefit from a workforce of highly skilled and talented people who want to make Nanaimo their home—a key factor in supporting a diverse and sustainable economy.

**Promoting a positive image** In order for Nanaimo to grow and move confidently into the future, local residents need to understand how special their city is. Feeling proud of their home, they project a positive image—and that positive image will attract more people and more businesses to the Harbour City.

With the Circle of Prosperity strategy firmly in place, the EDG has developed a number of highly successful initiatives to move the city into a bright economic future, including:

**The Business Retention and Expansion Program** Since 60 to 80 percent of new jobs are created by existing businesses, the EDG initiated BusinessCARE, a program focusing on retaining and expanding these businesses by identifying any obstacles they may face and finding solutions that will help them to grow.

**The Downtown Nanaimo Partnership** Composed of business people and leaders from the downtown area, this City

Council committee was created to help revitalize Nanaimo's downtown core.

**Film Nanaimo** This organization is building a film- and television-production industry in the central Vancouver Island area. Film Nanaimo markets the region as a production location, hosts location scouts and producers, and facilitates access to permits, experienced crew, and equipment.

**The Human Resources Strategy** This program addresses the workforce needs of the key sectors identified in the Economic Development Strategy. As EDG initiatives develop, critical skill gaps have been identified. The Human Resources Strategy pinpoints existing skill sets in the community and those that need to be developed.

The EDG has initiated many other strategies related to oil and gas exploration, shellfish farming, tourism, and other industries. The firm commitment and enthusiasm of this diverse volunteer group continue to ensure Nanaimo's prosperous future.

The Harbour City has a proud history and an exciting future. It is a community that boasts great natural beauty, a year-round temperate climate, bountiful economic opportunities, and friendly hospitable people.

Welcome to Nanaimo!

*Nanaimo's own town crier, Ray Parker, joins local RCMP officers on the dock to greet visiting cruise ship passengers.*

*Harbour nights, harbour lights.*

Goody Niosi was born in Karlsruhe, Germany, and immigrated to Canada at the age of five. After falling in love with books, she decided at age 10 that she would be a writer when she grew up. This is her third book.

Her first career was that of film editor in Toronto and Vancouver.

"What you do in your life gives you a partial picture of a person," Goody says. "To really know someone, ask them what their passions are. I am passionate about ideas and ideals."

*Magnificently Unrepentant*, the story of Merve Wilkinson and his sustainable logging career at Wildwood, was Goody's first book. In *Ordinary People, Extraordinary Lives*, she once again chose to tell stories of people who have made a difference in the world.

Goody writes for the *Nanaimo Daily News*, *Harbour City Star*, and other publications. She lives above a stable in the country with her dog, Lizzie the Labrabrat. When she is not outdoors or involved in various community activities, she can probably be found plunked down in front of her computer.

Terry Patterson was born in Manitoba and began his studies in photography at Camosun College in Victoria in 1977. After graduating he moved to Calgary, where he worked as a commercial photographer for four years. In 1985 he settled in Nanaimo, where he works with numerous corporate clients. He also runs a small image bank of the area.

"We live in such a great place that I hardly think of what I do as work or a job," Terry says. "You could be falling out of a tree and about to hit the ground and still get a nice photo." Terry lives just south of Nanaimo in rural Yellow Point with his partner Eve and her collection of assorted critters.